R s

HarperCollins*Publishers*

YOUR COLLINS TRAVELLER

Your Collins Traveller Guide will help you find your way around your chosen destination quickly and simply. It is colour-coded for easy reference:

The blue section answers the question 'I would like to see or do something; where do I go and what do I see when I get there?' This section is arranged as an alphabetical list of topics. It is recommended that an up-to-date atlas or street plan is used in conjunction with the location maps in this section. Within each topic you will find:

- A selection of the best examples on offer.
- How to get there, costs and opening times for each entry.
- The outstanding features of each entry.
- A simplified map, with each entry plotted and the nearest landmark or transport access.

The red section is a lively and informative gazetteer. It offers:

- Essential facts about the main places and cultural items.
  What is La Bastille? Who was Michelangelo? Where is Delphi?

The gold section is full of practical and invaluable travel information. It offers:

- Everything you need to know to help you enjoy yourself and get the most out of your time away, from Accommodation through Baby-sitters, Car Hire, Food, Health, Money, Newspapers, Taxis and Telephones to Youth Hostels.

PRICES (1993)	Inexpensive	Moderate	Expensive
Attractions			
Museums, etc.	under 300 Drs	300-500 Drs	500-1000 Drs
Restaurants			
Meal, exc. wine	1000-2000 Drs	2000-3000 Drs	over 3000 Drs
Nightclubs			
Entry and drink	under 1000 Drs	1000-2000 Drs	over 2000 Drs

Lindos

Cross-references:

Type in small capitals – **CHURCHES** – tells you that more information on an item is available within the topic on churches.

A-Z after an item tells you that more information is available within the gazetteer. Simply look under the appropriate name.

A name in bold – **Holy Cathedral** – also tells you that more information on an item is available in the gazetteer – again simply look up the name.

CONTENTS

CONTENTS

INTRODUCTION

Helios, the sun-god, fell in love with Rhodes when he saw her emerging from the waves after the great flood sent by Zeus. Mortals have been enchanted by 'the isle of the roses' ever since. The sun rules the whole island for about 300 days every year. Spring until late autumn is an almost unbroken chain of sunny days and balmy nights. Roses, hibiscus, bougainvillea, jasmine and honeysuckle flourish. The scent of Rhodes is unforgettable.

For the tourist the island can provide almost everything: swimming in beautiful bays; lazing on beaches of golden sand; drinking ouzo in waterfront cafés; watching the rich toy with their yachts; or exploring the maze of the Old Town of Rhodes. It's a relaxing place. There is little crime and not even a jail. Offenders have to catch the ferry to Kos, another Dodecanese island, to go to prison!

The best way to arrive is by boat, sailing between the statues of a stag and a hind on pillars at the entrance to Mandraki Harbour. If you don't have your own yacht, cheat a little. Take one of the many boat trips from Mandraki around the coast, even as far as Lindos, and imagine the return trip is the first time you have seen the harbour, one of the most romantic in the Mediterranean.

The Colossus of Rhodes, one of the Seven Wonders of the World, reputedly straddled the entrance to Mandraki. Scholars now say the statue could have been elsewhere in the town, but the setting is so perfect that you feel the story could be true. Mandraki itself, with windmills on one side, is dominated by the Old Town's honey-coloured walls, originally built in the Middle Ages by the Knights of St. John, and restored this century by occupying Italians inspired by Mussolini's dream of making the Mediterranean a Roman sea again.

Rhodes is one of the most cosmopolitan of the Greek islands. Modern Rhodes Town can compete with many European cities in its stock of designer label goods. Strangely for an island so dominated by the sun, there are also dozens of shops selling fur coats and umbrellas. The Old Town, hiding behind its thick walls, is a maze of streets and alleys. Narrow lanes between shuttered houses suddenly open up into tree-shaded squares with tavernas and bars. The main streets, once patrolled by armoured knights, are lined with shops and stalls selling ceramics, leather goods, paintings and souvenirs.

Lindos

Lindos is now a whitewashed tourist haunt but it was once the island's capital. The little town, with its sandy beach and the best natural harbour on the island, nestles under another fortress built by the Knights of St. John. Above the castle on the acropolis are the remains of a 4thC BC temple to Lindian Athena. You can also visit ancient Ialyssos and Kamiros which, with Lindos, predate the founding of Rhodes Town. Ialyssos has an underground shrine to St. George with beautifully restored frescoes depicting the life of Christ. Christianity mingles with other religions. There are remains of a Doric fountain and a temple to Athena and Zeus. Kamiros was abandoned at the time of Christ, after about five centuries of decline. The ruins of the ancient buildings have been excavated and tourist guides will tell you the remains are the Rhodian equivalent of Pompeii.

The valley of the butterflies at Petaloudes is a fascinating place; walk through and marvel at the brilliantly coloured creatures in their thousands, apparently asleep on the trunks of trees. Visitors are asked to go quietly and not to disturb them.

Since Helios began his affair with the island, there have been other suitors – and most of them have been rough. For 5000 years waves of invaders occupied the island. Among them were the Minoans from Crete who colonized the island and built shrines for bull worship. Warriors from Rhodes fought at Troy. In 305 BC Demetrius the Besieger, King of

Ancient Kamiros

Macedonia, spent almost a year trying to take the island's capital. He built a large siege tower ten storeys high with built-in grappling hooks and catapults. When the siege failed the defenders sold the siege engine and used the cash to pay for a massive statue of the sun-god. Completed by Charles of Lindos c.290 BC, the Colossus stood for 65 years until an earthquake caused it to buckle at the knees and fall. Tradition has it that the statue lay where it had fallen until the mid-17thC, when Arab raiders carried off the bronze and sold it for scrap in Syria.

Romans, Goths, Persians and Arabs all attacked the island in the centuries that followed. Eventually Rhodes was occupied by Genoese pirates from whom the Knights of St. John, in retreat from the Holy Land, bought the island. By the early part of the 14thC the Crusaders had begun their impressive fortifications. For more than 200 years they held the island against frequent attack, until they eventually surrendered, after a 145 day siege, to Sultan Suleiman the Magnificent and left for Malta. Four hundred relatively peaceful years followed.

After World War I, the Italians took over the Dodecanese, allegedly holding them in trust until they could be united with Greece. The new overlords also started excavating and restoring archaeological sites. By the 1930s their rule had become oppressive. They outlawed the Greek language and the Greek Orthodox religion. Rhodes was to be the play-

Rhodes Old Town

ground for their ruling classes. When Mussolini fell Germany occupied the islands until they were liberated by British troops in 1945. The Dodecanese were united with Greece in 1947.

Rhodes has plenty of history, ancient and modern, but the real treasure of the island is its people. Their generosity is famous. In one restaurant our eight-year-old daugther asked for melon, which was not on the menu. We told her she couldn't have it, but the waiter shrugged, said 'No problem', and sent one of his lads to a supermarket to buy one. He charged the same price as the supermarket too! Our six-year-old son was intrigued by a poster in a beach bar showing various cocktails. He wanted a gin fizz complete with umbrellas, fruit and sparklers. The waiter said 'No problem' and produced a 'ginless fizz' with all the trimmings for the cost of a Coke. The point is, neither needed to go to the trouble of pandering to the children, as we had practically convinced them they couldn't have their way.

Be prepared to answer questions about your family, home and job. Rhodians take the ancient law of hospitality seriously and show such an interest in the visitor that to a north European it may seem like prying. Don't be offended; be flattered by the interest shown. In Greek the word for stranger and guest is the same.

William McDowall

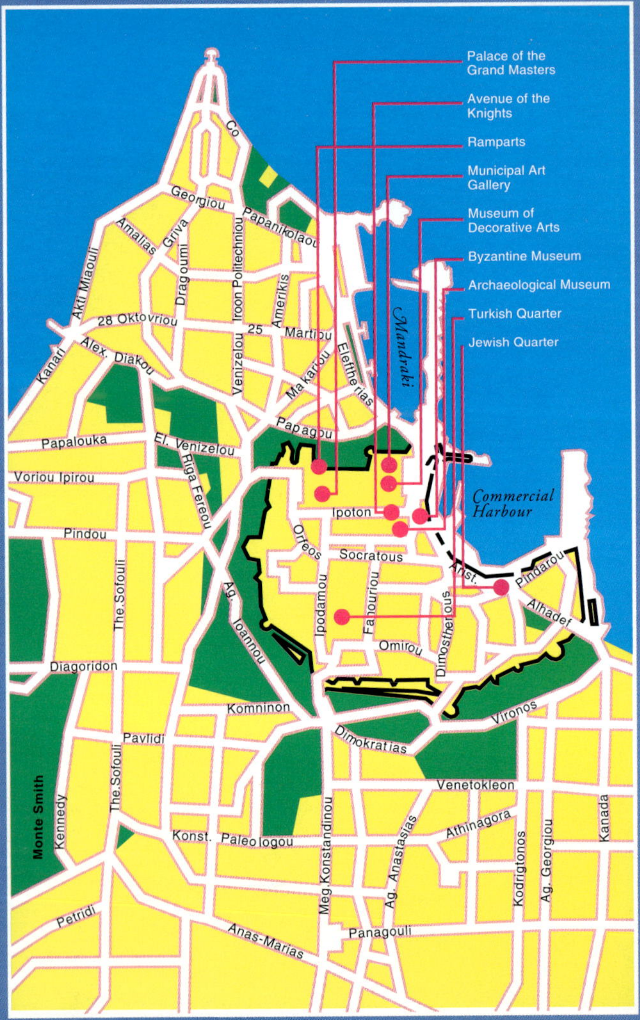
Palace of the Grand Masters
Avenue of the Knights
Ramparts
Municipal Art Gallery
Museum of Decorative Arts
Byzantine Museum
Archaeological Museum
Turkish Quarter
Jewish Quarter
Mandraki
Commercial Harbour
Georgiou
Papanikolaou
Amalias
Griva
Akti Miaouli
Dragoumi
Iroon Politechniou
Amerikis
28 Oktovriou
25 Martiou
Kanari
Alex. Diakou
Venizelou
Makariou
Eleftherias
Papagou
Papalouka
El. Venizelou
Riga Fereou
Voriou Ipirou
Ipoton
Orfeos
Pindou
Socratous
The.Sofouli
Ag. Ioannou
Ipodamou
Fanouriou
Dimosthenous
Arist.
Pindarou
Alhadef
Omirou
Diagoridon
Komninon
Vironos
Pavlidi
Dimokratias
Venetokleon
Monte Smith
Kennedy
Konst. Paleologou
Meg.Konstandinou
Ag. Anastasias
Athinagora
Kodrigtonos
Ag. Georgiou
Kanada
Petridi
Anas-Marias
Panagouli

PALACE OF THE GRAND MASTERS Platia Kleovoulou, Old Town. ▪ 0800-1900 Tue.-Sat., 0800-1500 Sun. ● Expensive. *More of a fortress than a palace. The home of the leader of the Knights. See* **A-Z**.

AVENUE OF THE KNIGHTS (ODHOS IPOTON) Old Town. *A narrow, cobbled street leading up to the Palace of the Grand Masters (see above). On either side are the Inns of the various orders of Knights. See* **A-Z**.

RAMPARTS Old Town. ▪ Guided tours 1445 Tue.-Sat. ● Expensive. *Superb fortifications built by the Knights. See* **Rhodes Old Town**.

ARCHAEOLOGICAL MUSEUM Platia Moussiou, Old Town. ▪ 0800-1900 Tue.-Sat., 0830-1500 Sun. ● Moderate. *A fine exhibition of archaeological finds, labelled in Greek and English.*

MUSEUM OF DECORATIVE ARTS Platia Argirokastrou, Old Town. ▪ 0800-1900 Tue.-Sat., 0830-1500 Sun. ● Moderate. *Beautiful furniture, pottery and costumes, and many items from Lindos. See* **A-Z**.

MUNICIPAL ART GALLERY Platia Simi, Old Town. ▪ 0800-1400. ● Moderate. *A modern building constructed in medieval style. Local artists are featured in modern art exhibitions.*

BYZANTINE MUSEUM Port end of Odhos Ipoton (see above), Old Town. ▪ 0800-1900 Tue.-Sat., 0830-1500 Sun. ● Moderate. *Once the Knights' (see* **A-Z***) cathedral, and a mosque under Turkish rule.*

TURKISH QUARTER Old Town. *The Turkish influence, which can be seen in numerous minarets and arched windows, dates from the 16thC. See* **WALK 2**, **A-Z**.

JEWISH QUARTER Old Town. *The prominent feature of this area (southeast part of the Old Town) is the fountain in the Square of the Jewish Martyrs topped by bronze sea horses. See* **WALK 2**.

Rhodes Town
Bay of Trianda
Kremasti
Ialyssos
Soroni
Maritsa
Faliraki
Kalithies
Salakos
Afandou
Bay of Afandou
Kritinia
Moni Tsambika
Embonas
Archangelos
Mount Ataviros
Agios Issidoros
Laerma
Monolithos
Moni Thari
Lardos
Lindos
Apolakkia
Lardos Bay
Apolakkia Bay
Genadi
Moni Skiadi
Katavia
Cape Prassonissi
RHODES TOWN
Cathedral of the Evangelist
Suleiman Mosque
St. Mary's Church

SULEIMAN MOSQUE Socratous Street, Rhodes Old Town. Closed to the public. *Built in honour of Suleiman the Magnificent after the Turkish conquest of 1522, it has beautiful, faded paintwork. There are good views of it from the adjacent clock tower. See* **A-Z**.

CATHEDRAL OF THE EVANGELIST Mandraki Harbour, Rhodes Town. 0730-1400, 1700-2030. Donation welcomed. *Built by the Italians in 1925 as a replica of the original Church of St. John, which was destroyed in 1856, the cathedral has an ornate interior.*

ST. MARY'S CHURCH Odhos Ipoton, Rhodes Old Town. *Now the Byzantine Museum (see* ATTRACTIONS 1*), the plain-ceilinged interior is an ideal setting for the frescoes, etc. exhibited here.*

IALYSSOS Filerimos, 13 km southwest of Rhodes Town. 0800-1740 Tue.-Fri., 0830-1440 Sat. & Sun. Church of Our Lady; Moderate. *Within the ancient city of Ialyssos are the Church of Our Lady of Filerimos, the underground Chapel of Agios Georgios with its restored 15thC frescoes, and a monastery with a Doric fountain. See* EXCURSION 1, **Filerimos**.

MONI THARI 4 km southwest of Laerma. Bus at 1500 to Laerma. Ask in village for caretaker (Mr Anestes). Donation welcomed. *Monastery in a beautiful setting in a hollow in the wooded hills. There are several picnic sites in the surrounding area. See* EXCURSION 4.

MONI SKIADI 3 km down an untarred road west of Messanagros. Bus at 1500. Donation welcomed. *Byzantine monastery in a superb setting, which was restored in the 18thC. Some interesting frescoes in the cupola. See* EXCURSION 4, **A-Z**.

MONI TSAMBIKA 29 km south of Rhodes Town, 2.5 km off the east coast road. 1.5 km up a steep road to the car park then a rough path and concrete steps. Donation welcomed. *This white Byzantine monastery with only five cells sits on a hill-top with superb views. It is the setting for an annual fertility-rite ceremony. See* EXCURSION 3, **A-Z**.

Rhodes Town
Bay of Trianda
Monte Smith
Kremasti
Ialyssos
Kalithea
Soroni
Maritsa
Faliraki
Petaloudes
Ancient Kamiros
Kalithies
Salakos
Afandou
Bay of Afandou
Kritinia
Embonas
Archangelos
Mount Ataviros
Agios Issidoros
Feraclos Castle
Laerma
Monolithos
Monolithos Castle
Lardos
Lindos
Apolakkia
Apolakkia Bay
Lardos Bay
Genadi
Katavia
Cape Prassonissi

LINDOS 56 km south of Rhodes Town on the east coast.
Acropolis: 0830-1840 Tue.-Fri., 0830-1445 Sat. & Sun. Expensive.
Quaint narrow streets, white houses, and the famed acropolis of Lindos. See EXCURSION 3, WALK 4, **A-Z**.

ANCIENT KAMIROS 34 km southwest of Rhodes Town on the west coast. 0800-1740 Tue.-Fri., 0830-1440 Sat. & Sun. Moderate.
A huge excavated site. The main street leads uphill to the Temple of Athena, and on either side are the alleyways of houses. See EXCURSION 2, **A-Z**.

PETALOUDES 25 km southwest of Rhodes Town.
0830-1700 June-Sep. Inexpensive June-Sep., Free rest of year.
A wooded valley which is home to hundreds of brightly coloured butterflies. See EXCURSION 1, **A-Z**.

MONOLITHOS CASTLE 2 km from Monolithos, 80 km southwest of Rhodes Town. Daily bus, but check on Sun. Free.
Ruined castle on a rocky outcrop. The sweeping views are majestic, but beware of the unguarded 260 m drop. See EXCURSION 2, **A-Z**.

MONTE SMITH 2 km west of Rhodes Town. Free.
The site of the main visible Classical remains of ancient Rhodes Town, named after the British admiral who used the area as a lookout point. See **A-Z**.

FERACLOS CASTLE 40 km south of Rhodes Town on the east coast. Free.
Used by the Knights (see **A-Z***) as a fortress/prison, this was the last fortification to fall to the Turks. There are impressive views of the coastline. See* EXCURSION 3, **A-Z**.

KALITHEA 12 km south of Rhodes Town. Free.
A spa built by the Italians in the 1920s in Arabic style, though the mineral springs' healing powers have been known since ancient times. Now rather run down. See BEACHES 1, EXCURSION 3, **A-Z**.

Rhodes Town
Bay of Trianda
Ialyssos
Kremasti
Soroni
Maritsa
Kalithea
Faliraki
Kalithies
Afandou
Bay of Afandou
Salakos
Kritinia
Embonas
Mount Ataviros
Tsambika
Archangelos
Stegna
Agios Issidoros
Haraki
Laerma
Monolithos
Kalathos
Vliha
Lardos
Lindos
Pefka
Apolakkia
Apolakkia Bay
Lardos Bay
Genadi
Katavia
Cape Prassonissi

KALITHEA 10 km south of Rhodes Town. Frequent buses.
Good swimming in the clear water from three adjacent coves near to the old spa. There are showers on the beach and toilets in the spa building, as well as a food kiosk in season. See EXCURSION 3, **A-Z**.

FALIRAKI 16 km south of Rhodes Town. Frequent buses.
There are several access points to this 3.5 km beach which has large hotels along its northern section. Facilities include showers, loungers for hire, tavernas and water sports. See EXCURSION 3, **A-Z**.

AFANDOU 21 km south of Rhodes Town. Regular buses.
Long, wide, pebble and sand beach. Tavernas and cantinas. See **A-Z**.

TSAMBIKA 31 km south of Rhodes Town. Regular buses.
Sheltered, sandy beach with food, drink and pedalos available in season.

STEGNA 36 km south of Rhodes Town, 3.5 km from Archangelos.
An attractive, undeveloped village strung out along a clean, sandy beach, with a small harbour for fishing boats.

HARAKI 42.5 km south of Rhodes Town. Some buses in high season.
A sheltered beach with tavernas reached through olive groves, and dominated by the ruins of Feraclos Castle (see ATTRACTIONS 3*).*

KALATHOS 49.5 km south of Rhodes Town.
A long, shingle beach, still largely undeveloped.

VLIHA 54 km south of Rhodes Town.
Good sheltered beach. Less crowded than Lindos. Refreshments in hotels.

LINDOS 56 km south of Rhodes Town.
A wide, sandy beach with clear water. Crowded in high season. See **A-Z**.

PEFKA 5 km south of Lindos.
A sheltered, sandy beach with showers, and umbrellas for hire. There has been some villa development. There are tavernas in the village.

Rhodes Town
Bay of Trianda
Ialyssos
Kremasti
Soroni
Maritsa
Faliraki
Kalithies
Afandou
Bay of Afandou
Salakos
Kritinia
Embonas
Mount Ataviros
Archangelos
Glifadas
Agios Issidoros
Laerma
Monolithos
Fourni
Lardos
Lindos
Apolakkia
Glystra
Kiotari
Lardos Bay
Apolakkia Bay
Genadi
Katavia
Cape Prassonissi
Plimiri

GLYSTRA 13 km south of Lindos, at south end of Lardos Bay.
Undeveloped sandy beach backed by dunes and pine trees. Cantina.

KIOTARI 18.5 km south of Lindos.
Fine shingle/coarse sand beaches with showers and good swimming, although the beaches shelve steeply. Tavernas and bicycle rental kiosks.

GENADI 22 km south of Lindos.
Sand and shingle beaches which stretch 10 km but shelve steeply. There are three tavernas, plus showers and bicycle rental. *See* **EXCURSION 4**.

PLIMIRI 36 km south of Lindos.
Fine shingle beach with a jetty used by the locals for fishing. Taverna.

CAPE PRASSONISSI 49.5 km south of Lindos. At Katavia turn off down a rough track for 8 km.
Beautiful expanse of sand between the island and mainland. Only advisable in calm weather; otherwise deserted. Taverna. *See* **A-Z**.

APOLAKKIA BAY Approximately 80 km south of Rhodes Town.
A huge expanse of undeveloped pebbly beach with superb views. There are several access points between Katavia and Apolakkia. *See* **A-Z**.

FOURNI 75.5 km south of Rhodes Town.
Access to this secluded, undeveloped, sandy beach with nearby caves is from Monolithos. *See* **EXCURSION 2**.

GLIFADAS 47 km south of Rhodes Town, 6 km from the main road.
A remote, rocky beach with a taverna and rooms to rent.

IALYSSOS 9 km south of Rhodes Town.
Sand and pebble beach with tavernas. Loungers and umbrellas for hire.

RHODES TOWN From Aquarium to Elli Beach and outer harbour.
Sand and pebbles, and good swimming. Showers, refreshments. Pedalos, umbrellas and loungers for hire. Very crowded but rather exposed.

Rhodes Town
Rodini Park
Bay of Trianda
Trianda
Kremasti
Filerimos
& Ialyssos
Pastida
Maritsa
Eleousa
Kalithies
Petaloudes
Psinthos
Afandou
Bay of Afandou
Archangelos

EXCURSION 1

A half-day excursion round the north of the island.

Take the main road west out of Rhodes Town.
8 km – Trianda. Now more commonly known as Ialyssos. Continue along the road past a stretch of hotels and modern buildings to arrive at the site of the most ancient remains on Rhodes. Visit the picturesque church of Theotokos (Mother of God) with its intricately carved icons. Turn left out of Trianda town centre and follow the winding road for 5 km up to Filerimos, site of the ancient city of Ialyssos (see **ATTRACTIONS 2**). After visiting the church, chapel and monastery, return to the entrance, cross the car park and follow the stations of the Cross along a shady walk to a viewpoint looking out to Paradisi and Kremasti. Return to Trianda and turn left along the coast road.
16 km – Kremasti (see **A-Z**). The modern Byzantine-style church was donated to the village by American expatriates. It can be visited if you track down the caretaker. This is also the site of several necropolises. Turn left off the coast road after 6 km (the turning is well-signposted) and fork right after another 1 km.
23 km – Petaloudes (see **ATTRACTIONS 3**, **A-Z**). Leave your car in the car park at the lower entrance to the valley. The valley is usually very busy so try to get there early. After seeing the butterflies, continue in a south-easterly direction towards the village of Psinthos. The road from Petaloudes to Psinthos is rough in places but passes through dramatic mountainous countryside.
28 km – Psinthos. Site of a fierce battle earlier this century between the Turks and the Italians, ending nearly four centuries of Turkish rule. Continue towards Afandou but after 6 km fork left to Kalithies.
38 km – Kalithies. There is an impressive view of Mount Psalida on the right. To the north of the village is Eleousa Monastery, whose church is decorated with interesting frescoes. Check in the village whether the monastery is open. Continue through a modern industrial area on the outskirts of Rhodes Town then turn left through a tunnel in the rock into Rodini Park.
50 km – Rodini Park (see **A-Z**). The park is little-visited by tourists and is pleasantly peaceful. There are peacocks, an enclosure with deer, a children's playground and the Tomb of the Ptolemies.

Rhodes Town
Ialyssos
Kremasti
Soroni
Kamiros
Skala
Kamiros
Castle
Makri
Strongli
Ancient
Kamiros
Profitas
Ilias
Kolimbia
Eleoussa
Apolona
Embonas
Mount Ataviros
Siana
Monolithos
Fourni
Monolithos
Castle
Lindos
Apolakkia

Monolithos

A one-day excursion along the west coast of the island.

Take the west coast road through Ialyssos (see **ATTRACTIONS 2**) and Kremasti (see **A-Z**) and past the airport to Kalamonas.
23 km – Soroni. The village is famous for its donkey races held on 30 July in honour of St. Soulas. Continue along the coast road, bearing right to Kalavarda, and turn left after 4 km.
27 km – Ancient Kamiros (see **ATTRACTIONS 3**, **A-Z**). The excavations give an excellent idea of what the city looked like, even though there is no interpretative information on site. You can, however, buy a guide-book at the ticket kiosk or hire a guide (available in high season; price depends on number in group). Spend some time exploring the site and then return to the main road and perhaps choose a beach-side taverna for a coffee.
40.5 km – Kamiros Skala (see **A-Z**). A pleasant place to have a meal or drink. This is also the last place you'll be able to buy petrol on this excursion route. Turn right off the main road approximately 2 km beyond Kamiros Skala and follow the untarred road.
44.5 km – Kamiros Castle. Also known as Kritinia Castle. The outer walls of the castle are in good repair but inside there is little to see apart from lizards sunning themselves on the rubble. However, there are splendid views of the neighbouring uninhabited islands of Makri and Strongli. Rejoin the main road south, bypassing the villages of Kritinia and Amartos.
64 km – Siana. Goblets with black figures dating from 6 BC were found in the necropolis here. The village is totally unspoilt, so it's probably a good idea to continue driving in order to keep it that way.
68 km – Monolithos. Continue south through the pine forest from this small village perched on the slopes of Mount Acramytis. Follow the track for 2.5 km to Monolithos Castle (see **ATTRACTIONS 3**, **A-Z**) with its amazing views of the sea and surrounding countryside. Leave the car in the car park and walk up the stone steps to the castle. Inside is a tiny whitewashed chapel and the remains of the barrel vault of an earlier chapel. Drive another 4 km down the untarred road to Fourni beach (see **BEACHES 2**) and the man-made caves in the limestone cliffs where Christians hid from the Arabs in the 7thC. Return to Monolithos village

Monolithos

and Siana. Continue beyond Siana for 10.5 km then turn right for Embonas.

87.5 km – Embonas (see **A-Z**). The centre of the grape-growing region and one of the most picturesque villages on Rhodes. You can find guides who will lead you up Mount Ataviros (see **A-Z**) here. Continue north for 9 km then turn right. Take the mountain road through pine trees past Alpine-style hotels (built for Italian commanders during the occupation) on Profitas Ilias (see **A-Z**). In spring the area is carpeted with tiny white and pink anemone flowers. Return to the main road, follow it for 1 km, then turn left for Apolona. The road to Apolona and Eleoussa is extremely scenic, with pine-covered slopes which open out onto walnut and olive groves. At several points there are picnic areas with rustic tables and chairs.

127 km – Eleoussa. At the centre of the village is an impressive yellow-washed colonnaded square. Unfortunately the village is occupied by the military and no photographs are allowed. From Eleoussa, take a right turn and follow the road along the wide Loutani valley to the main east coast road at Kolimbia. Turn left to return to Rhodes Town.

Rhodes Town
Kremasti
Kalithea
Faliraki
Psinthos
Afandou
Eleoussa
Kolimbia
Epta Piges
Archangelos
Moni Tsambika
Feraclos Castle
Kalathos
Lindos

EXCURSION 3

Lindos

A one-day excursion along the east coast of the island.

Take the east coast road from Rhodes Town signposted to Lindos. After 10 km turn left to Kalithea (see **ATTRACTIONS 3**, **A-Z**). Return to the main road.

15.5 km – Faliraki (see **BEACHES 1**, **A-Z**). A busy beach resort with water-sport facilities. After 5 km turn right off the coast road for 2 km.

22.5 km – Afandou (see **A-Z**). This bustling village is the centre of the carpet-weaving industry on the island, although there is otherwise little to see. On the other side of the main road is the turn for the beach (see **BEACHES 1**) and the golf course. Along the road to the course are the beginnings of a leisure complex planned to include a swimming pool, tennis courts, hotels and restaurants. Rejoin the main road south.

28.5 km – Kolimbia & Epta Piges (see **A-Z**). Turn right and follow the road alongside the usually dry riverbed of the Loutani valley. After 2 km, take a steep left turn up a cement road to a shady taverna, and a car park where raucous peacocks often strut. The tunnel entrance is next to the river. Follow it, ankle-deep in beautifully cold fresh water (not for the claustrophobic) through to the bright, blue-green lake which is fed by seven streams (hence Epta Piges). Return to Kolimbia and follow the road south. Moni Tsambika (see **ATTRACTIONS 2**, **A-Z**) is well worth a visit, though its spectacular hill-top location makes access quite difficult. Turn left at the signpost and a tarred road leads to the car park, from where steps lead to the monastery.

37 km – Archangelos (see **A-Z**). One of the Rhodian ceramic-producing centres. The village has a pleasant old quarter and a 15thC castle. Return to the main road and turn left after 4 km.

42 km – Feraclos Castle (see **ATTRACTIONS 3**, **A-Z**). One of the strongest castles of the Knights (see **A-Z**), with panoramic views, though little of it now remains. Access is by a rough track. Turn left 2 km after turning off the main road. Return to the main road and turn left towards Lindos. About 4 km beyond Kalathos the road sweeps round to the right, giving a dramatic view of Lindos Bay and the acropolis towering above it.

60 km – Lindos (see **ATTRACTIONS 3**, **WALK 4**, **A-Z**). Park at the top of the hill in the designated car parks (no charge). Return to Rhodes Town on the main road or continue with **EXCURSION 4**.

Eleoussa
Embonas
Laerma
Monolithos
Moni Thari
Apolakkia
Profilia
Lardos
Lindos
Vatio
Arnitha
Pefka
Moni
Skiadi
Genadi
Messanagros
Katavia
Cape
Prassonissi

Cape Prassonissi

A one-day excursion round the southern part of Rhodes.

Take the small road south out of Lindos, curving round Mount Marmari. Notice the tiny white chapel situated in the pass. After the left turn to Pefka (see **BEACHES 1**) after 4 km, the road begins to get potholed. On the left is Lardos Bay with several sandy beaches.
8 km – Lardos. See the ruins of the medieval castle. Take the north road out of Lardos, following the signs for Laerma. The road takes a scenic route, winding gently up a wooded hill-side. In spring the slopes are covered with wild flowers, including orchids.
20 km – Laerma (see **A-Z**). A picturesque hill village. Enquire here for the caretaker of Moni Thari (see **ATTRACTIONS 2**). Take the rough untarred road out of the village to the southwest, following the signs to Profilia. After 2 km take the turn for the monastery, which lies 2 km down a rough track. The road between Moni Thari and Profilia is very bad so return to Lardos and follow the coast road south. The road passes numerous pleasant sandy beaches, all less crowded than those in the more developed north of the island.
38 km – Genadi (see **BEACHES 2**). Last of the east coast resorts. Just before the village three windmills, one converted into a villa, can be seen near the road-side. After Genadi the coastal plain widens out into a fertile agricultural area. Between Genadi and Katavia there is evidence of the Italian occupation, with large, abandoned, fortified buildings, some with towers and churches.
57 km – Katavia. The 14th-15thC church has 17thC frescoes, and remains dating from the pre-Christian era have been found near the village. There are tavernas and a petrol station. From here rough tracks lead to the island's most southerly point. After 8 km there are breathtaking vistas of the causeway linking the cape with the mainland.
65 km – Cape Prassonissi (see **BEACHES 2**). Take the windswept causeway to the island, weather permitting, where a track leads past Italian fortifications to the lighthouse. Return to Katavia and turn left up the unsurfaced road to Messanagros. The road is rough and precipitous in places and should only be attempted by the confident. There are spectacular views beyond Messanagros which make the drive worth the effort. The road to Moni Skiadi (see **ATTRACTIONS 2**, **A-Z**) is better but

not well signposted. Return the 3 km to Messanagros and turn left for Arnitha and Apolakkia. The road is unpaved and rough, climbing along the Koukouliari ridge, from where panoramic views of both coasts are possible. Continue through Arnitha to the main road and turn left for Apolakkia.

104 km – Apolakkia (see **BEACHES 2**, **A-Z**). A small, thriving village surrounded by citrus and walnut groves. The Church of Agios Georgios Vardas on the outskirts of the village is said to be the oldest church in the Dodecanese (see **A-Z**). Retrace your route for 2 km and then follow the road through Vatio to Genadi, where you rejoin the main road back to Lindos.

Cape Prassonissi

FISHERMEN
OFFICE

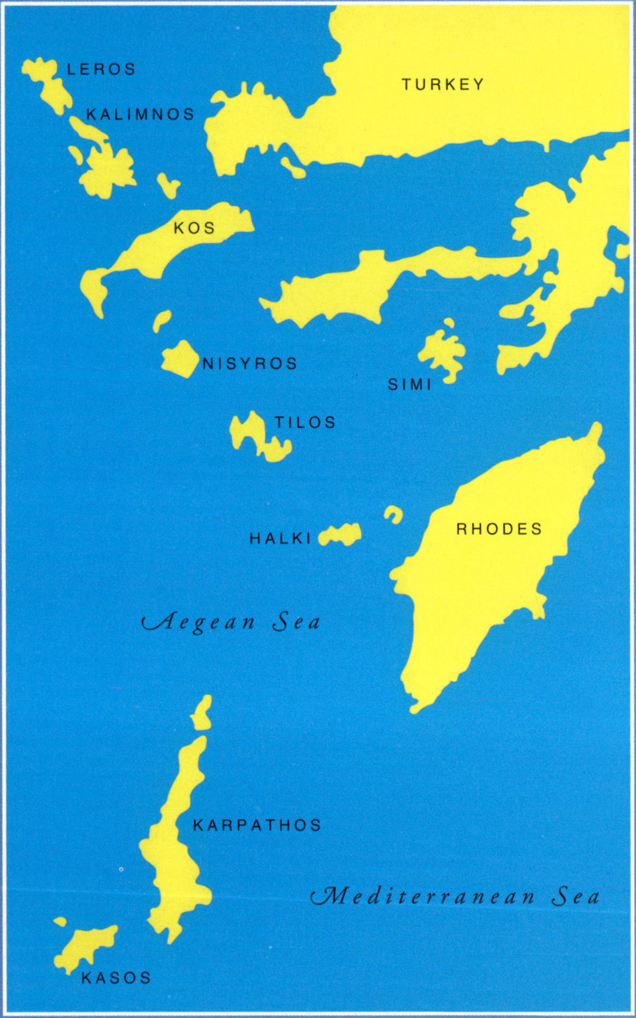
LEROS
KALIMNOS
TURKEY
KOS
NISYROS
SIMI
TILOS
HALKI
RHODES
Aegean Sea
KARPATHOS
Mediterranean Sea
KASOS

SIMI 40 km northwest of Rhodes.
Daily boat services (1 hr 15 min). Hydrofoil (30 min) is expensive.
A pleasant day trip. The main port is a site of historic interest. See **A-Z**.

HALKI 10 km west of Rhodes.
Three boats per week from Rhodes Town. Daily service from Kamiros Skala.
The closest island to Rhodes. Quiet, with pleasant beaches. See **A-Z**.

TILOS 75 km west of Rhodes.
Three ferries per week.
A developing tourist island with a strong folk history. See **A-Z**.

NISYROS 100 km west of Rhodes.
Three boats per week in summer.
The island has an active volcano and a lush green landscape. See **A-Z**.

KOS 100 km northwest of Rhodes.
Daily ferries (4 hr). Hydrofoil service. Summer flights from Rhodes.
Second only to Rhodes as a Dodecanese holiday destination. See **A-Z**.

KALIMNOS 135 km northwest of Rhodes.
One boat per week, though more in summer (6 hr).
A mountainous island with olive groves and orchards. See **A-Z**.

LEROS 150 km northwest of Rhodes.
Daily boat in summer (7 hr). Flights from Rhodes Mon., Wed. & Fri.
Another mountainous island with beautiful countryside. See **A-Z**.

KARPATHOS 50 km southwest of Rhodes.
Three ferries per week (7 hr). Daily flights from Rhodes (35 min).
Good beaches, fertile valleys, rugged mountains, few tourists. See **A-Z**.

KASOS 170 km southwest of Rhodes.
Three boats per week (10 hr). Six flights per week (30 min).
A scenic island with few tourist amenities. See **A-Z**.

Minuit Club
Casino
Zorba
Zum
Bouzio's
Mandraki
Commercial Harbour
Panorama Bar
Café Chantant
Copacabana
Georgiou
Papanikolaou
Amalias
Griva
Akti Miaouli
Dragoumi
Iroon Politechniou
Amerikis
28 Oktovriou
25 Martiou
Kanari
Alex. Diakou
Venizelou
Makariou
Eleftherias
Papagou
Papalouka
El. Venizelou
Riga Fereou
Voriou Ipirou
Ipoton
Pindou
Orfeos
Socratous
Arist.
Pindarou
Alhadef
The. Sofouli
Ag. Ioannou
Ipodamou
Fanouriou
Dimosthenous
Omirou
Diagoridon
Komninon
Vironos
Pavlidi
Dimokratias
Venetokleon
Monte Smith
Kennedy
Konst. Paleologou
Meg. Konstandinou
Ag. Anastasias
Athinagora
Kodrigtonos
Ag. Georgiou
Kanada
Petridi
Anas-Marias
Panagouli

CASINO Grand Hotel Astir Palace, New Town.
2000-0300. Expensive.
In a smart, new building, this is one of only three casinos in Greece. Roulette and baccarat. Evening wear and passport obligatory for entry.

BOUZIO'S Elli Club buildings, Platia Koundourioti, New Town.
2200-0230. Expensive.
Greek and international music with artistes from all over Greece. Young clientele of various nationalities.

PANORAMA BAR Platia Ippocratous (Sindrivani Square), Old Town. 2000-0230. Expensive.
Friendly bar in picturesque setting on second- and third-floor terraces. Well decorated with an abundance of plants. A good vantage point for watching the nightlife in the square.

CAFÉ CHANTANT Off Platia Ippocratous (Sindrivani Square), behind the Panorama Bar (see above). 2230-0300. Expensive.
Greek music in atmospheric bar. Extremely popular with young Greeks.

COPACABANA 4 Australias Street. 2100-0230. Moderate.
Lively atmosphere. Singers from Rhodes and the Greek mainland are showered with carnation petals in appreciation. Mainly Greek clientele.

MINÚIT CLUB 6 Kastelorizou Street. 2200-0230. Moderate.
Very popular. Friendly staff, and a lively atmosphere. A good mix of ages and nationalities. Greek music and folk dancing display at 2400.

ZUM Georgiou Papanikolaou, New Town.
1900-0100. Moderate.
A noisy, lively music and cocktail bar. Very popular with Scandinavians.

ZORBA Iroon Politechniou Street, New Town.
2100-0230. Moderate.
Informal atmosphere, Greek food and some dancing. Within walking distance of the town centre. Very popular with the locals.

Co
Piccolo
Georgiou
Papanikolaou
Amalias
Griva
Aris
Akti Miaouli
Dragoumi
Iroon Politechniou
Amerikis
Mandraki
28 Oktovriou
25 Martiou
Kanari
Alex. Diakou
Venizelou
Makariou
Eleftherias
Papagou
Kon Tiki
Papalouka
El. Venizelou
Voriou Ipirou
La Maison Fleurie
Riga Fereou
Commercial Harbour
Ipoton
Alexis
Casa Castellana
Pindou
Orfeos
Socratous
Plaka
Arist.
Pindarou
Argo
Alhadef
The. Sofouli
Ag. Ioannou
Ipodamou
Fanouriou
Dimosthenous
Omirou
Diagoridon
Komninon
Vironos
Pavlidi
Dimokratias
Venetokleon
Monte Smith
Kennedy
The.Sofouli
Athinagora
Kanada
Konst. Paleologou
Meg.Konstandinou
Ag. Anastasias
Kodrigtonos
Ag. Georgiou
Petridi
Arapaki
Anas-Marias
Panagouli
La Pizzagio

See **Opening Times**.

ALEXIS Socratous Street, Old Town. Expensive. *Mezes, fresh fish and seafood are served in this luxurious restaurant in a small courtyard.*

KON TIKI Floating platform, Mandraki Harbour. Expensive. *A floating seafood restaurant which is very expensive but worth it for the setting.*

LA MAISON FLEURIE Riga Fereou Street, Old Town, opposite Amboise Gate. Expensive. *French cuisine. Reasonable food but the room lacks atmosphere.*

CASA CASTELLANA 33 Aristotelous Street, Old Town. Expensive. *International menu and succulent seafood dishes served in a 15thC Knight's (see* **A-Z***) house enclosed by ramparts.*

ARGO Platia Ippocratous (Sindrivani Square), Old Town. Expensive. *Steaks and seafood in a lovely setting above the busy square.*

PLAKA Platia Ippocratous (Sindrivani Square), Old Town. Moderate. *Friendly proprietor and superb views over the Old Town walls. Fresh seafood.*

LA PIZZAGIO Platia Kostaridi on Kanada, New Town. Moderate. *Try this popular pizza and pasta house for a culinary change.*

ARAPAKI Themistokli Sofouli. Moderate. *Authentic Greek food. Serves some dishes not available elsewhere, such as good rice dishes.*

ARIS 46 Georgios Leontos Street, New Town. Moderate. *The emphasis here is on Greek food. Friendly staff.*

PICCOLO 9 Kastelorizou Street, New Town. Moderate. *A wide variety of international dishes and a trio of musicians to provide atmosphere. Caters mainly for Scandinavians.*

Loukoulos
Dolce Italia
Tzaki
Odyssey
Kamares
Hippocrates
Pythagora
Tsampicos
Mandraki
Commercial Harbour
Georgiou
Papanikolaou
Amalias
Griva
Dragoumi
Iroon Politechniou
Amerikis
Akti Miaouli
28 Oktovriou
25 Martiou
Alex. Diakou
Kanari
Venizelou
Makariou
Eleftherias
Papagou
Papalouka
El. Venizelou
Riga Fereou
Voriou Ipirou
Ipoton
Pindou
Orfeos
Socratous
Arist.
Pindarou
Alhadef
The. Sofouli
Ag. Ioannou
Ipodamou
Fanouriou
Omirou
Dimosthenous
Diagoridon
Komninon
Vironos
Pavlidi
Dimokratias
Venetokleon
Monte Smith
Kennedy
Athinagora
Konst. Paleologou
Meg. Konstandinou
Ag. Anastasias
Kodrigtonos
Ag. Georgiou
Kanada
Petridi
Anas-Marias
Panagouli

See **Opening Times**.

ODYSSEY 10-12 Menekleous Street, Old Town. Moderate.
Greek dishes, charcoal dishes and fresh fish served on a pleasant terrace in an atmospheric street setting in the Old Town.

TSAMPICOS Kavoyrakia Beach, 10 min by car or taxi from Rhodes Town on the Kalithea road. Moderate.
Fresh seafood is served in this family-run beach taverna. Popular with tourists from the local hotels and with Greeks at weekends.

PYTHAGORA 22 Pythagoras Street, Old Town. Moderate.
A roomy family-run taverna with a cheerful atmosphere and fresh seafood.

HIPPOCRATES Pythagoras Street (off Platia Ippocratous), Old Town. Moderate.
Greek food served at tables set out along the alleyway. Popular locally.

KAMARES 47-49 Agios Fanouriou, Old Town. Moderate.
Taverna serving Greek food in attractive surroundings. Off the main tourist trail but just a brief walk from busy Socratous Street.

LOUKOULOS 33 Amerikis Street, New Town. Moderate.
A varied Greek menu served in a small shady garden sheltered from the noises of the street. Street-side tables are also available.

DOLCE ITALIA 18 Alex. Diakou Street, New Town. Inexpensive.
Italian ices and cappuccino served where you can watch the world go by. A good place to enjoy a mid-morning break.

TZAKI 5 km from Rhodes Town at Ixia on the west coast road. Inexpensive.
Reasonable prices and popular with tourists from nearby hotels, though frequented by Greeks too. Live Greek music in the evening.

Rhodes Town
Bay of Trianda
Ialyssos
Kremasti
Paradise Taverna
Soroni
Maritsa
Faliraki
Kalithies
Blue Sea
Afandou
Taverna Afandou
Bay of Afandou
Salakos
Johnny's Fish Taverna
Kritinia
Taverna Tsampikos
Embonas
Archangelos
Mount Ataviros
Agios Issidoros
Laerma
Monolithos
Hermes
Lardos
Lindos
Taverna Lardos
Apolakkia
Lardos Bay
Stefanis
Genadi
Antony's
Apolakkia Bay
Katavia
Cape Prassonissi

See **Opening Times**.

HERMES Lindos. On the left on entering the Old Town. Expensive. *Away from the bustle, with a roof-top terrace overlooking the bay. Excellent Greek and international food.*

STEFANIS Kiotari Beach, Asklipios. Moderate. *Family-run taverna specializing in fish, with a shady terrace above the road with views of the small harbour and nearby beaches.*

ANTONY'S Genadi. Moderate. *Taverna-cum-fish restaurant on beach. Choose lobster from the tank or favourite dish from the kitchen.*

PARADISE TAVERNA Faliraki. At the extreme south of the bay. Moderate. *Very good Greek restaurant on the outskirts of the unsightly sprawl of Faliraki. Excellent moussaka, souvlakia and fish.*

JOHNNY'S FISH TAVERNA Kamiros Skala. Take the first right beyond Kamiros Skala, signposted Johnny's. Moderate. *Above a tiny fishing cove, with fine views. Fish and grills.*

BLUE SEA Old Kamiros. On the right just before the village. Moderate. *There's a wide variety of seafood at this beach-side restaurant, but a good selection of grills and salads too.*

TAVERNA AFANDOU Afandou Beach. Just before the military area. Moderate. *Family-run. Service can be very slow, but the* calamaries *are fresh and the Greek salad perfect.*

TAVERNA LARDOS Lardos Beach. Between the main road and the beach. Moderate. *All kinds of hot and cold foods, including fish dishes and Greek specialities. Draught lager and bottled beers and wines.*

TAVERNA TSAMPIKOS Stegna. Midway along the waterfront. Inexpensive. *Delightful Greek café. Old men play backgammon, there's lots of laughter, and good Greek salad and coffee.*

Mocassino
Astero
Meletiou Brothers Trading Company
Lalounis
Stergos Marias
Nikos & Takis
Trik-Mai-Fort
Panagiotis Loukidis
Teheran Carpets
Mandraki
Commercial Harbour
Georgiou
Papanikolaou
Amalias
Griva
Dragoumi
Iroon Politechniou
Amerikis
Akti Miaouli
28 Oktovriou
25 Martiou
Kanari
Alex. Diakou
Venizelou
Makariou
Eleftherias
Papagou
Papalouka
El. Venizelou
Riga Fereou
Voriou Ipirou
Ipoton
Pindou
Orfeos
Socratous
Arist.
Pindarou
Alhadef
The.Sofouli
Ag. Ioannou
Ipodamou
Fanouriou
Dimosthenous
Omirou
Diagoridon
Komninon
Vironos
Pavlidi
Dimokratias
Venetokleon
Monte Smith
Kennedy
The.Sofouli
Konst. Paleologou
Meg.Konstandinou
Ag. Anastasias
Athinagora
Kodrigtonos
Ag. Georgiou
Kanada
Petridi
Anas-Marias
Panagouli

See **Opening Times**.

TRIK-MAI-FORT 14 Alex. Diakou Street, New Town.
Interesting collection of imported and locally-made jewellery, paintings, antiques, studio pottery and glassware.

MOCASSINO 28 Oktovriou Street, New Town.
High-quality men's and women's shoes, as well as handbags. Prices compare favourably with similar quality goods on sale in the UK.

PANAGIOTIS LOUKIDIS 7 Orfeos Street, Old Town.
Reproduction Byzantine art, including icons and Byzantine-inspired jewellery in gold and silver inlaid with precious and semiprecious stones.

ASTERO 1 Fanouriou Street, Old Town. *Shop selling copperware, including pots and decorated plates. Some rare pieces of work from the Dodecanese. Very reasonable prices though open irregular hours.*

MELETIOU BROTHERS TRADING COMPANY 62a Ermou Street, just off Platia Ippocratous, Old Town. *Moderately-priced, good-quality wooden craftware, some in Turkish style.*

LALOUNIS Platia Moussiou, Old Town. *The famous Athens jeweller, with a select choice of very high-quality pieces, mainly inspired by or reproductions of ancient Greek artefacts. Cheaper than the Paris or Zurich shops but still very expensive. Wonderful medieval atmosphere.*

TEHERAN CARPETS 42b Aristotelous Street, Old Town.
Carpets and rugs from all over the Middle East, from homespun Greek cotton and wool to fine Persian silk. Helpful English-speaking staff.

STERGOS MARIAS 4 Panetiou Street, Old Town. *Jeweller's which sells a selection of fossils, crystals and semiprecious stones. Expensive.*

NIKOS & TAKIS Panetiou Street, Old Town.
Quality clothing with a flavour of Rhodes in both design and colours.

Gallurakis
Christos
Paneri
H. Mevloutaki
Mandraki
Photographic Museum
Hartofilis
Cosmos
Royal Mink
Phidias
Commercial Harbour
Co
Georgiou
Papanikolaou
Amalias
Griva
Dragoumi
Iroon Politechniou
Amerikis
Akti Miaouli
28 Oktovriou
25 Martiou
Kanari
Alex. Diakou
Venizelou
Makariou
Eleftherias
Papagou
Papalouka
El. Venizelou
Riga Fereou
Voriou Ipirou
Pindou
Ipoton
Orfeos
Socratous
Arist.
Pindarou
Alhadef
Ipodamou
Fanouriou
Dimosthenous
Omirou
The.Sofouli
Ag. Ioannou
Diagoridon
Komninon
Vironos
Dimokratias
Pavlidi
Venetokleon
Athinagora
Monte Smith
Kennedy
Konst. Paleologou
Meg.Konstandinou
Ag. Anastasias
Kodrigtonos
Ag. Georgiou
Kanada
Petridi
Anas-Marias
Panagouli

See **Opening Times**.

PANERI 1 Fanouraki Street, New Town.
Health foods, organically-grown produce, Greek herbs and natural cosmetics. The proprietor is a friendly Greek-American.

GALLURAKIS 100 Griva Street, New Town. *A wide selection of leather goods (bags, belts, sandals, etc.) at very reasonable prices.*

CHRISTOS Griva Street, New Town.
Watercolours of the Rhodian countryside and sights displayed in a garden courtyard. Customers can enjoy a drink while browsing.

ROYAL MINK Apellou Street, just off Platia Moussiou, Old Town.
Traditional-design rugs and carpets. A weaver works on the premises.

PHIDIAS Panetiou Street, Old Town.
Pottery from Athens hand-painted by Costas Peppas. Both antique copies and his own inspirations are on sale.

H. MEVLOUTAKI 149 Socratous Street, Old Town. *A shop in a busy bazaar area of the Old Town selling leather sandals of every description.*

HARTOFILIS 81 Socratous Street, Old Town.
Shop selling embroidered articles from all over Greece and Cyprus, and blouses from Rhodes. Handkerchiefs, tablecloths, table mats and napkins, each showing the technique from a particular region.

PHOTOGRAPHIC MUSEUM 2 Ermou Street, by the Marine Gate, Old Town. 1000-1400 Mon.-Fri. *Not really a museum at all, but more a bookshop selling guides, posters, and reproductions of old plates, maps, charts and drawings of Rhodes. An interesting place to browse.*

COSMOS 62 Ermou Street, just of Platia Ippocratous, Old Town.
High-quality furs, leather clothing and jewellery sold in this shop, which has a friendly and knowledgeable proprietor.

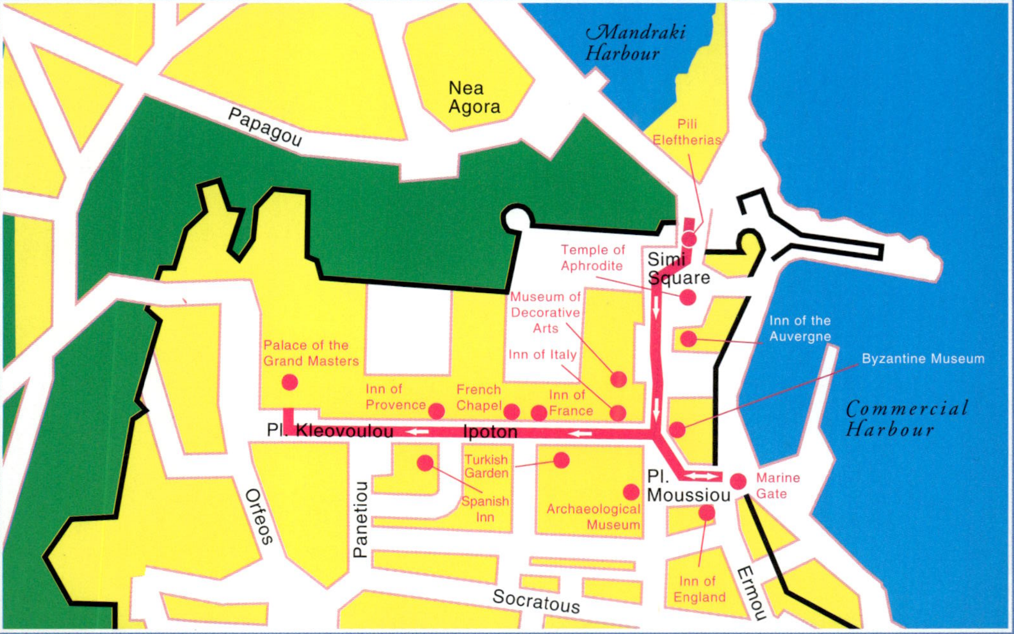
Mandraki Harbour
Nea Agora
Papagou
Pili Eleftherias
Temple of Aphrodite
Simi Square
Museum of Decorative Arts
Inn of the Auvergne
Byzantine Museum
Commercial Harbour
Palace of the Grand Masters
Inn of Italy
Inn of Provence
French Chapel
Inn of France
Pl. Kleovoulou
Ipoton
Turkish Garden
Spanish Inn
Archaeological Museum
Pl. Moussiou
Marine Gate
Orfeos
Panetiou
Socratous
Inn of England
Ermou

WALK 1

The Knights' Quarter

Duration: 3 hr.
From Mandraki Harbour (see **A-Z**) enter the city through the Pili Eleftherias (Gate of Freedom). This gate is approached across the moat where a herd of Rhodian deer can be seen. Opposite the gate, at the other end of Simi Square, are the remains of a temple to Aphrodite, and behind this is the Inn of the Auvergne. This was built in the 15thC and renovated around 1919, and overlooks Platia Argirokastrou. In the centre of the square is a Byzantine font which forms the base of a fountain topped by a small dolphin. All round the square are mounds of stone cannonballs dating from the 15thC. The Institute of History and the Museum of Decorative Arts (see **A-Z**) are also located here. Pass under an arch and you will see on the left the Byzantine Church of St. Mary, which houses the Byzantine Museum (see **ATTRACTIONS 1**). Leaving Odhos Ipoton on the right, continue to Platia Moussiou and the Inn of England, founded in 1482. On the left stands the impressive Marine Gate, through which can be seen the commercial harbour. This 15thC gate bears the coat of arms of the Grand Master Pierre d'Aubusson. Opposite is the Hospital of the Knights, founded in 1440, which now houses the Archaeological Museum (see **ATTRACTIONS 1**). Retrace your steps and turn left up the Avenue of the Knights (see **A-Z**), or Odhos Ipoton, which leads to the palace. The buildings were sympathetically restored in the early part of this century exactly as they were in medieval times, and the cobbled street is very atmospheric. Along this street are four of the remaining six Inns (see **A-Z**). On the left is the north façade of the hospital, and opposite, the Italian Inn. Further along on the right is the Inn of France, the most elegant of all, and next to it is the small French chapel with a statue of Our Lady with the Saviour, and the French Lilies. Across from the Inn of France, behind a wrought-iron gate, is a cool, shady Turkish garden. Next to the Inn of France is the Inn of Provence, and opposite, the Inn of Spain. Pass under the arch to arrive at the castle square, Platia Kleovoulou. This used to be the site of the Church of St. John, destroyed by an explosion when gunpowder was ignited by a lightning strike. The Palace of the Grand Masters (see **A-Z**) is on the right, and ahead the square opens onto Orfeos Street and the Turkish Quarter (see **A-Z**), which is where **WALK 2** commences.

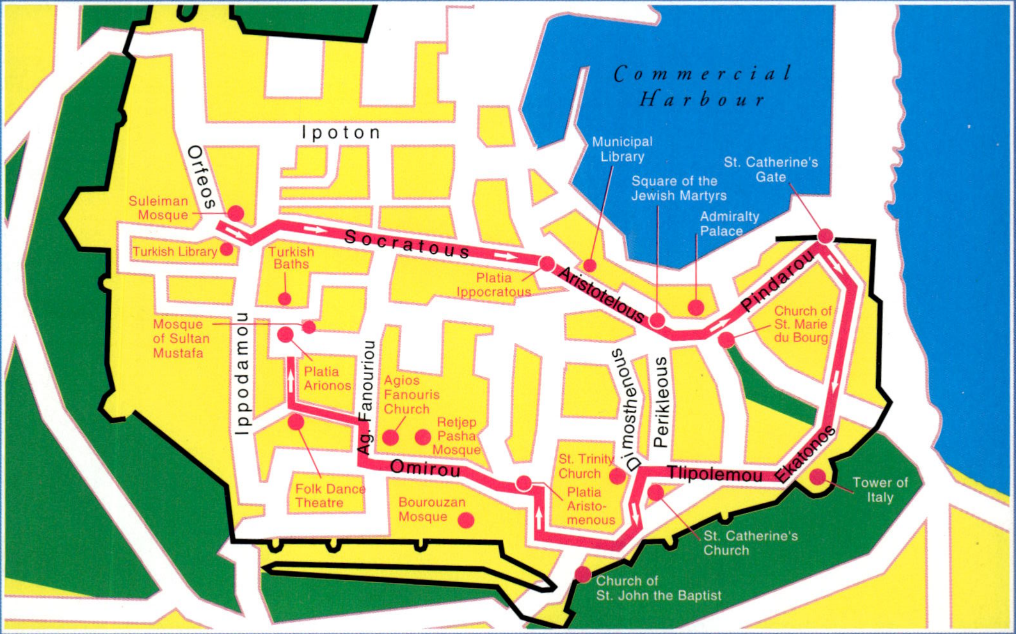
Commercial Harbour
Ipoton
Orfeos
Suleiman Mosque
Turkish Library
Turkish Baths
Socratous
Platia Ippocratous
Municipal Library
Square of the Jewish Martyrs
St. Catherine's Gate
Admiralty Palace
Aristotelous
Pindarou
Church of St. Marie du Bourg
Mosque of Sultan Mustafa
Ippodamou
Platia Arionos
Ag. Fanouriou
Agios Fanouris Church
Retjep Pasha Mosque
Dimosthenous
Perikleous
Omirou
St. Trinity Church
Platia Aristo-menous
Tlipolemou
Ekatonos
Tower of Italy
Folk Dance Theatre
Bourouzan Mosque
St. Catherine's Church
Church of St. John the Baptist

The Old Town

Duration: 2-3 hr.

Start at the Suleiman Mosque (see **A-Z**). Opposite is the Turkish Library, which contains a 15th/16thC Koran with illuminations, and is surrounded by a small paved garden. Follow Socratous Street, the old bazaar, where houses and shops still keep something of the Turkish atmosphere, downhill to Platia Ippocratous. At the far side of the square is the Municipal Library, with intricately decorated first-floor windows. At the centre of the square is a fountain, decorated with green and blue tiles, and topped by a statue of an owl. Now take Aristotelous Street, which leads to the Square of the Jewish Martyrs, where the Germans rounded up all the Jews in 1944 and deported them. In the centre is a fountain decorated with bronze sea horses. The Admiralty Palace, the former residence of the archbishop, stands on one side of the square. Pindarou Street passes the ruins of the Gothic Church of St. Marie du Bourg and the Hospice of St. Catherine before arriving at St. Catherine's Gate. The gate overlooks the busy commercial harbour. Walk towards the Tower of Italy and follow the ramparts west along Ekatonos Street and Tlipolemou Street. This will take you past the small 14thC Church of St. Catherine (a Byzantine church converted into a mosque by the Turks but now a church again). Opposite St. Catherine's Church is St. Trinity Church, an unusually-shaped 15thC church which was also once a mosque. Turn left past the latter church towards the city ramparts, where you will see the small Church of St. John the Baptist in the walls. Turn right into Platia Aristomenous. Here, excavations have revealed the remains of a mill, with several millstones visible. Bear left towards the delapidated St. Kyriaki Church (renamed Bourouzan). Follow Omirou Street. A walk along this narrow thoroughfare gives some flavour of the Turkish Quarter (see **A-Z**) and is a pleasant escape from the main tourist trail on Socratous Street. Opposite No. 31 is a gateway leading to the Retjep Pasha Mosque, once very grand, but now run down and closed. Opposite is Agios Fanouris Church, with 13th and 15thC frescoes. Cross over Agios Fanouriou Street and turn right towards the open-air Folk Dance Theatre (see **Culture**). The street opposite the entrance leads to Platia Arionos. On the left are the Turkish Baths and on the right the Mosque of Sultan Mustafa.

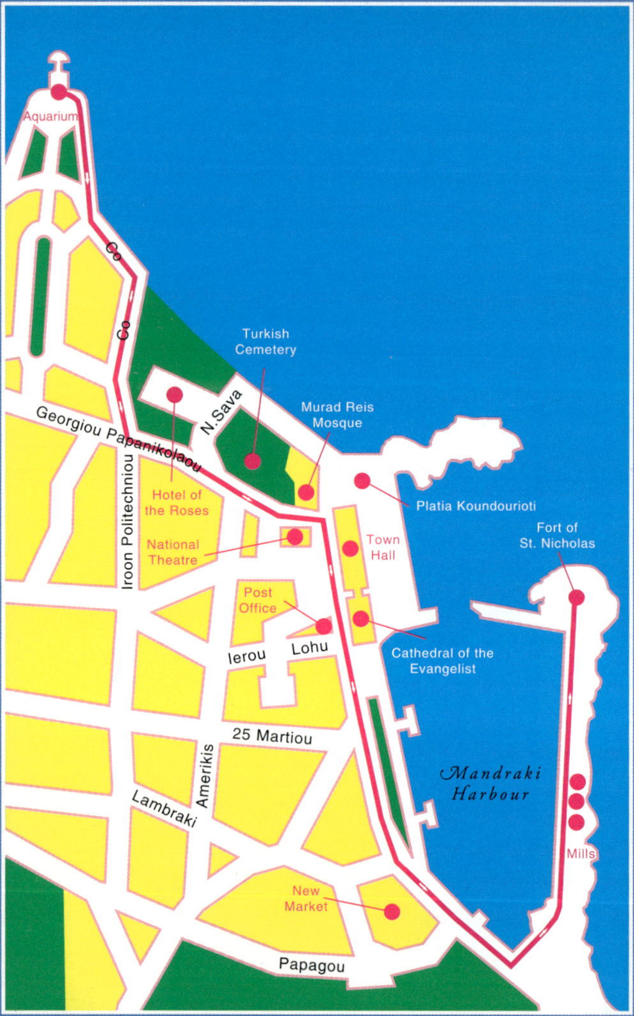
Aquarium
Co
Co
Turkish Cemetery
N.Sava
Murad Reis Mosque
Georgiou Papanikolaou
Hotel of the Roses
Platia Koundourioti
Iroon Politechniou
National Theatre
Town Hall
Fort of St. Nicholas
Post Office
Ierou
Lohu
Cathedral of the Evangelist
25 Martiou
Amerikis
Lambraki
Mandraki Harbour
Mills
New Market
Papagou

The New Town

Duration: 3 hr.
Start at the Aquarium (see **A-Z**) in the gardens on the northern tip of the island. Take the Co road along the beach on the northeast side of the town. The road leaves the beach and runs alongside gardens in which is the abandoned Hotel of the Roses. This once-luxurious hotel was built during the Italian occupation, and it was here that the peace treaty between Israel and Egypt was signed in 1979. Today it lies empty. Turning left into Vas Konstantinou will lead you to the gates of the hotel, and then to the Turkish Cemetery next to the tiny Murad Reis Mosque. Murad Reis was the naval commander of the Turkish fleet during the 1522 siege and the mosque is just big enough to hold his tomb. The cemetery contains graves of various notable characters, many of whom were exiles in Rhodes, for example, viziers, pashas, a shah of Persia and the poet Mohammed Ahmed Ephendi. Tombstones with a turban are those of men, plain ones those of women. The cemetery is now somewhat neglected but is shady and peaceful. Lawrence Durrell's (see **A-Z**) villa is to be found on the corner. Leaving the cemetery onto Platia Koundourioti, you enter the Mandraki Harbour (see **A-Z**) area. The entrance of the harbour is marked by two columns bearing bronze deer – the emblem of Rhodes. This was supposedly the site of the Colossus of Rhodes (see **A-Z**), though it is more likely to have been at the acropolis at Monte Smith. Walking down Eleftherias Street along the seafront, you will pass the grandiose harbour buildings. On the right is the National Theatre, which sometimes serves as a cinema, and opposite is the Town Hall, built in impressive Venetian Gothic style and which was once used as the Governor's Palace. On the left is the square bell tower of the Cathedral of the Evangelist (see **ATTRACTIONS 2**). The fountain at the front is a replica of Viterbo. Opposite is the post office and further down on the right are the city courts. Moored along the harbour are large yachts, some available for charter. This is also where several of the boats for the islands leave from, and there are stalls and small boats offering sponges for sale. Finally you will arrive at the New Market (see **A-Z**), a huge heptagonal building in Turkish style enclosing a courtyard with cafés, shops and stalls. Walk along the jetty, past three mills that used to grind the flour for the medieval cargo ships. At the end of the jetty is the Fort of St. Nicholas, now a lighthouse.

Tomb of Kleouboulus
Grand Harbour
Stone Cisterns
Bas-relief of Greek Galley
Acropolis
Donkey Station 2
Doric Columns
St. Paul's Bay
Chapel
Temple of Lindian Athena
Knights' Castle
Steps to the Acropolis
Church of Panaghia
Viewpoint
Stavri Sq.
Main Square
Information Kiosk
Donkey Station 1
Amphitheatre
Parking
Necropolis

Lindos

Duration: 2 hr.
Start from the information kiosk in the main square. This is the setting-down point for cars and coaches, which are not allowed in Lindos (see **A-Z**), and this is therefore the point at which most people enter the village. Go down the lane at the south end of the square. On the right is the donkey station. To hire a donkey for the ride up to the acropolis will cost 600 Drs each way. If you decide to walk, follow the signs for the acropolis. About 100 m on the left is the beautiful whitewashed Byzantine Church of Panaghia, with its distinctive bell tower and red-tiled domes. The church is in daily use and visitors are asked to dress respectfully when entering the church. The plainness and simplicity of the courtyard contrasts strongly with the richness of the decorated interior. The walls are completely covered with frescoes, and on the east wall are icons decorated with silver, gilt and jewels. Continue along the lane to the foot of the path to the acropolis. All the streets are lined with tourist shops selling embroidery and jewellery. This is also a good place to look back onto the medieval houses clustered in a maze of lanes and alleys. Just below the acropolis women sell tablecloths spread out under the trees. The entrance to the acropolis (admission 800 Drs) has a paved area with massive stone cisterns for grain or water. At the foot of the steps up to the fortress is a huge Greek galley carved in relief in the rock. Go up the stairs into the acropolis. There are a mass of stone remnants in various states of preservation and restoration. The most prominent features are the Doric columns (c.208 BC) and the remains of the Temple of Lindian Athena. Unfortunately, long-term restoration work means that the columns are almost permanently covered in scaffolding. Return towards the steps through the buildings added by the Knights (see **A-Z**) in the 15thC, when the acropolis was turned into a fortress, and turn right immediately after the ticket booth, past the donkey station. Walk down the path to the village, which gives wonderful views over Lindos Bay and the Grand Harbour. Visible on the headland on the opposite side of the bay is a circular stone tomb with a burial chamber. It is said to be the tomb of Kleouboulus, ruler of Lindos in the 6thC. From the path steps lead down to the beach, but continue to the village. You will pass some fine carved doorways, typical of the medieval houses of Lindos. Many of

Temple of Lindian Athena

the houses have patterned black and white pebbled floors and patios (*chochlaki*). At the Church of Panaghia walk south along the main shopping street of Lindos, which is also the location of most of the tavernas and bars in the town. Turn left at the National Bank in a small square at the end of the street and then first right along a lane which leads, in about 50 m, to an ancient stone amphitheatre carved into the hill slope. This is a superbly atmospheric, well-preserved site. Another 50 m further on, there are dramatic views from the road of the nearby circular St. Paul's Bay, with the acropolis towering above. The bay, reputed to be where St. Paul landed on the island, has a pleasant small beach and a tiny chapel. Follow the road along the length of the bay and turn back uphill to Platia Stavri. From here you get the best overall view of Lindos. Take the first left and follow the lane that skirts the hill of the necropolis, on the western edge of the village, back to the main square.

Afandou: 20 km from Rhodes Town. The town could not be seen off the coast by marauding pirates; hence the name Afandou, which means 'invisible'. The main industry of this commercial town is carpet-weaving. There is a pleasant beach nearby (see **BEACHES 1**). Also in the district is the only golf course on the island (see **Sports**). See **EXCURSION 3**.

Ancient Kamiros: 34 km from Rhodes Town. On the west coast road, this is one of the three ancient cities of Rhodes and the only one built without fortifications. It has been extensively excavated and the ruins give an excellent idea of the layout of the original city. The ruins include the agora (marketplace) with its Doric stoa (colonnade) from the 3rdC BC, an aqueduct and the Temple of Kamira Athena, next to which can be found the Panaghia Monastery. See **ATTRACTIONS 3**, **EXCURSION 2**.

Apolakkia: 91 km from Rhodes Town. One of the most southerly inhabited spots on the west coast of the island. The Church of Agios Georgios Vardas on the outskirts of the village is said to be the oldest church in the Dodecanese (see **A-Z**). See **BEACHES 2**, **EXCURSION 4**.

Aquarium: The aquarium is at the northern tip of Rhodes Town, off Kalymnou Lerou by the sea. There are interesting displays of common Mediterranean fish, live sponges, shellfish and octopus. 0900-2100; Moderate. See **WALK 3**.

Archangelos: 33 km from Rhodes Town. One of the larger villages on the island, Archangelos is located on the east coast road in a fertile area which is the main citrus fruit-growing region. The town itself has an atmospheric old quarter which lies in the shadow of a 15thC fortress commissioned by Grand Master Orsini. See **EXCURSION 3**.

Astipelea: The most westerly of the Dodecanese (see **A-Z**), in a remote position between Kos (see **A-Z**) and the Cycladic island of Amorga. The main town, also called Astipelea, sits on the island's central isthmus and has a number of chapels, a castle and beaches.

Avenue of the Knights (Odhos Ipoton): Rhodes Town. Restored to reflect its original appearance from the time when the Knights of St. John (see **Knights**) were the rulers of Rhodes, this cobbled street contains no shops and no traders. At one end is the restored Palace of the Grand Masters (see **A-Z**) which dates from the 14thC, and at the other is the Hospital of the Knights. Along the street's length are Inns (see **A-Z**) which were the quarters of each of the seven sections of the Knights (with the exception of England and the Auvergne). These sections were known as Tongues. Each represented a different part of medieval Europe, and was responsible for defending a different section of the ramparts (see **ATTRACTIONS 1**). See **WALK 1**.

Bouzouki: Bouzouki music has experienced a revival over the last 30 years. The instrument was brought to Greece in the 1920s by refugees from Asia Minor. It was banned for a time, though there were several underground bouzouki clubs in Athens. Today bouzouki characterizes Greek music, especially the old songs known as *rebetika*.

Cape Prassonissi: 91 km from Rhodes Town. This is the most southerly point on the island. A path leads for 8 km from the main road then over the sandy causeway to reach the rugged, windswept point with its view of the lighthouse. See **BEACHES 2**, **EXCURSION 4**.

Colossus of Rhodes: This 40 m statue, dedicated to the people of Rome, was considered one of the Seven Wonders of the World. It was destroyed by an earthquake in 225 BC. Controversy still rages as to where it stood: was it in the Temple of Zeus at the acropolis of Rhodes or did it bestride the entrance to Mandraki Harbour (see **A-Z**)?

Dodecanese: The name means '12 islands' but the group is actually made up of 14 main islands. They are closer to Turkey than to Greece and in ancient times were more influenced by the events of Asia Minor than by Athens or Sparta. Achaeans, Porians, Crusaders, Turks, Italians and Germans have all occupied the islands, which were not united with Greece until after World War II. In addition to Rhodes, the main group of islands includes Kos, Kalimnos, Leros and Patmos, which have regular ferry links to Piraeus and an interisland hydrofoil service. The smaller islands – Karpathos, Kastelerizo, Halki, Simi, Tilos, Nisyros, Astipelea, Telendos and Lipsi – are served by local ferries or excursion boats. Kos, Rhodes and Leros have airports. See **ISLANDS** and individual **A-Z** entries.

Durrell, Lawrence (1912-1990): The poet and author Lawrence Durrell spent two years on Rhodes at the end of World War II, helping to set the island back on its feet after the German occupation. He lived in a tiny villa at the corner of the Turkish Cemetery (see **WALK 3**) in Rhodes Town, which is now marked by a small brass plaque. Sadly in need of love and attention and not open to the public, the villa is nevertheless worth a look from the outside. Durrell wrote much of *Reflections on a Marine Venus* (1953) here, which gives a fascinating account of the island as it will never be again.

Embonas: 35 km from Rhodes Town. A picturesque village situated on the northwest slopes of Mount Ataviros (see **A-Z**) in a tobacco- and grape-growing region. Tavernas in the area serve jugs of the local wine. Here you will also find guides for the ascent of Mount Ataviros. The other local tradition is the permanent dance troupe of villagers in traditional costume who participate in both small village fêtes and larger national ones. At Embonas performances are organized during the last three weeks of Aug. See **EXCURSION 2**.

Epta Piges (Seven Springs): 30 km from Rhodes Town. The site of a reservoir fed by seven streams, and a man-made waterfall designed to provide water for the irrigation canals of Kolimbia, which were introduced by the Italians in the 1930s. The area is scenic and popular with tourists. See **EXCURSION 3**.

Faliraki: 15 km from Rhodes Town. One of the island's most popular resorts and the location of many large hotels. The long beach (see **BEACHES 1**) has full water-sports facilities, including water-skiing. It is possible to visit the ceramics factory of Neofitou, which produces up to 1200 pieces a day and also has a shop. See **EXCURSION 3**.

Feraclos Castle: 25 km from Rhodes Town. Near the village of Haraki, these are the ruins of one of the medieval fortresses built by the Knights (see **A-Z**) and used as a gaol for both war and civil prisoners. To the north are the remains of ancient tombs and a church, Aghia Agatha, which is decorated with 15th and 17thC frescoes. See **ATTRACTIONS 3**, **EXCURSION 3**.

Filerimos: 13 km from Rhodes Town. On the west coast road, this is the site of the Doric city of Ialyssos, one of the three ancient cities of Rhodes. It was the landing point of invading forces, and was also the location of the country residences of rich Venetian merchants, Knights (see **A-Z**) and Ottoman Turks in later centuries. The acropolis dominates the area and shows why it was such a strategic position. From the Classical period one can see the Temple of Athena and Zeus Polieus (4thC BC), built in Doric style on the foundations of the sanctuary, probably of Phoenician origin. On the left the underground Chapel of St. George boasts some restored mural paintings of the 14th and 15thC. On the right the baptismal font of an early Christian church marks the way to the restored Church of Panagia of Filerimos, part of the monastery founded by the Knights of St. John. Further up the road are the ruins of a castle of the Knights. See **ATTRACTIONS 2, EXCURSION 1**.

Halki: A mountainous island with few roads which is sparsely inhabited apart from two villages. Niborio is the principal village and is sited round the harbour. Although there are no hotels, accommodation is available in private houses. The nearest beach is Pandemos, a 10 min walk beyond the hill behind the town. Chora, 4 km from Niborio, was a flourishing centre in the 18th and 19thC but is now practically deserted. The medieval castle, with the ruins of a church behind it, offers a magnificent view from its location above the village. Access to Halki is by boat from Kamiros Skala. There are usually daily sailings at 1500 but times vary at the discretion of the boat owners. The trip takes 1.5 hr and the price is negotiable with the boatman, but is approximately 3000 Drs. Don't forget to check for times of return sailings. See **ISLANDS**.

Ialyssos: See **ATTRACTIONS 2, BEACHES 2, EXCURSIONS 1 & 2**.

Inns: Rhodes Town. Each of the seven Tongues of the order of the Knights of St. John (see **Knights**) had its own residence which was known as an Inn. Five of these Inns were located on the Avenue of the Knights (see **A-Z**). The Inn of France is the best-preserved example and has an interesting façade with an off-centre doorway decorated with coats of arms. It is occasionally used as a recital hall. Next door is the Inn of Spain, built in a style that reflects Catalan influence. The Inn of Italy was restored during the period of Italian occupation to resemble the original building. The Inn of Provence was a later addition to the avenue, dating from the early 15thC and having a less ornate façade than the others. Nothing remains of the Inn of Germany but a plane tree to mark the site. The Inn of England is situated on Platia Moussiou and was originally built in 1493, but was destroyed by an earthquake in 1851, rebuilt by the Italians in 1919 and further restored by the British after World War II. The Inn of the Auvergne is also situated away from the Avenue of the Knights, on Platia Simi. Today it houses state offices. See **WALK 1**.

Ixia: 3 km south of Rhodes Town. On the west coast, this village has been swamped by a series of hotel complexes which date back to the 1960s.

Jewish Quarter: Rhodes Town. See **ATTRACTIONS 1**, **WALK 2**.

Kalimnos: The island's principal town is Pothea, with its colourful houses, animated market and a local museum with displays on how early-20thC Greeks lived. Sponge-fishing is a main industry and the local sponge factory takes in organized visits. North of Pothea is the Cave of the Seven Virgins, with various inscriptions and votive alcoves. The beautiful beach at Vathy, 6 km north of Pothea on the east coast, is served by a regular bus service. See **ISLANDS**.

Kalithea: 10 km from Rhodes Town. The mineral springs and thermal waters here have been known for their healing properties since ancient

times. Hippocrates recommended them for kidney disorders, rheumatism and arthritis. The thermal baths were built by the Italians in 1929 but are now sadly delapidated. A series of arches encircles a spring at the back of the bay, and the baths themselves are paved in black and white pebbles. There is also a small, pleasant beach (see **BEACHES 1**). The site retains a certain charm. See **ATTRACTIONS 3, EXCURSION 3.**

Kamiros Skala: 48 km from Rhodes Town. This village was formerly known as Kritinia, as it was founded by Cretan sailors. There is a small quay for fishing boats and ferries to and from Halki (see **A-Z**). There are also three tavernas, and this is a regular coach stop. See **EXCURSION 2.**

Karpathos: Pigadia is the main port and located nearby are the remains of an ancient city. The island has few tourist facilities. Arkassa lies 10 km southwest of Pigadia and has a good beach, and the remains of a Byzantine church. There are charming villages throughout the island but these have to be visited on foot as there are practically no roads. See **ISLANDS.**

Kasos: Fry is the small capital town and contains an art museum and the monastery of Agios Mamas. Within walking distance are two intriguing caves – Ellino Kamares, which is partially concealed by a Hellenistic wall, and Selia, which is more natural, with stalagmites and stalactites. There are bus links to various picturesque beaches and towns around the island. See **ISLANDS**.

Kastelerizo: Close to the Turkish coast, this island still has a distinctly Greek flavour. Accommodation is cheap, delicious seafood is available, and there is a tiny but interesting museum located in an old mosque. There are also the remains of a Knights' (see **A-Z**) castle. Parasta Cavern is a worthwhile excursion. Free sailings leave from Mandraki Harbour as the Greek government is trying to develop tourism on the island.

Knights: The Knights of St. John of Jerusalem (or Knights of Rhodes, and later Malta) formed in the 11thC as a charitable brotherhood to take care of the poor and sick pilgrims in the Hospital of Jerusalem, built by the merchants of Amalfi. They soon became a military order, sworn to defend the Holy Sepulchre and fight the Muslims. They became the rivals of the Knights Templar and were obliged to retire to Cyprus and from there to Rhodes, which they took by force after a two-year siege. The order consisted of soldiers, chaplains and serving brothers, who followed the soldiers into action. The order was later divided into seven sections representing the seven languages or Tongues, each of which had a bailiff. The Council of Bailiffs was presided over by the Grand Master, elected for life by the Knights. For two centuries they fought the invading Turks successfully but were finally forced to surrender the island in 1522 after a long siege. The Grand Master and 180 survivors left for Crete and from there went to Malta in 1530. See **Avenue of the Knights**, **Inns**.

Kos: Kos is considered to be the second major island of the Dodecanese (see **A-Z**) group. Kos Town is of diverse historical interest, with archaic, Classical, Hellenistic and Roman remains. The most striking remains are the Castle of the Knights of St. John (see **Knights**), which was built during the 15th and 16thC using materials from the ruins of an ancient acropolis on the same site (0900-1530 Wed.-Sat., 0930-1430 Sun.; Inexpensive). Kos Town Hall features a turreted clock tower and mosaic entrance, and is a magnificent example of Italian architecture. It is now an administrative building for the police and courts. Also to be seen is the Casa Romana, a 3rdC house which has remarkable mosaic floors and frescoes. There are numerous pools, rooms and courtyards, with the ruins of a once-impressive Hellenistic mansion in the gardens (0900-1500 Mon.-Sat., 0930-1430 Sun.; Inexpensive). Hippocrates was born on Kos and the Archaeological Museum contains a famous statue of him which was found at the Odeon of Kos. The ancient sanctuary of Asclepion was the site of Hippocrates' 5thC BC medical school – the first in the world. Built on five levels on a hill behind the town, it includes Roman baths, the elegant Temple of Apollo, and minor and major temples of Asclepion. The archaeological site near the waterfront at Agora has a temple of Aphrodite, a temple of Hercules and a Roman basilica. Beaches round Kos Town tend to be extremely crowded. Continue round to Lampi on the northern tip of the island for a quiet beach. Thermi, with its black sand and pebbles, is a good beach with hot springs which make the sea warm. The best beach on the island is 5 km east of Kamani in the south. Kos can be visited in one day but merits a rather longer stay. All types of accommodation are available. See **ISLANDS**.

Kremasti: 5 km from Rhodes Town. Some of the most beautiful examples of geometric and archaic vases to be seen in the Archaeological Museum in Rhodes Town (see **ATTRACTIONS 1**) were found in the necropolises around Kremasti. Of interest in the town itself is the small church leaning against the ruins of a medieval castle. There is also a large modern church in Byzantine style which was paid for by villagers who had emigrated to the USA. See **EXCURSIONS 1 & 2**.

Laerma: 30 km from Rhodes Town. The village nearest to the geographical centre of the island. It is approached from Lindos and the east coast via a picturesque drive through woodland, much of which has been destroyed by fire. Nestling in the valley 4 km southwest of the village is the 9thC monastery of Moni Thari (see **ATTRACTIONS 2**). The monastery has a 13thC Byzantine church with a cupola and original wall paintings, covered over in parts by 16th and 17thC paintings. The church's beautiful icons include one of St. Michael, to whom the monastery is dedicated. See **EXCURSION 4**.

Leros: The main town of Platanaos is built on the side of a hill crowned with a Byzantine fortress which was restored by the Knights of St. John (see **Knights**). A road leads from the town to the port of Lakki. The best beaches on the island are the clean, sandy and usually deserted ones at Gourna and Vromolithios. There is a good taxi service on the island and some buses, but cycling is the best means of transport. See **ISLANDS**.

Lindos: 56 km from Rhodes Town. On the east coast, Lindos is the second town and one of the three ancient cities of Rhodes. This beautiful town is dominated by a steep hill, on which sits the acropolis of Lindos. The town itself is grouped around two small bays which make naturally safe harbours. There are some medieval houses, with many Arab influences, but most houses date from the 16thC. The streets are paved with black and white pebbles in traditional motifs, and some passages are decorated with mosaics. The doorways, intricately carved and painted, add to the charm of the town. The ancient acropolis is enclosed by walls within which are the 13 restored columns of the Doric stoa (200 BC), which stand in front of the stairs leading up to the 4thC BC Temple of Lindian Athena. There is a superb view from here and the walk up is not too strenuous if taken at a gentle pace. Donkey rides are available part of the way (0800-1700 Mon.-Sat., 0900-1700 Sun.; 600 Drs each way). Further sites of interest include the Crusader fortress on the rock 125 m above the town, and the Church of the Assumption of the Madonna, which was rebuilt in 1489 and houses colourful 18thC frescoes, and lies between the town and the acropolis. In addition to the sites of antiquity, there are some of the finest stretches of beach on the island to the south of the town (see **BEACHES 1**). Lindos can become very crowded with visitors in high season. See **ATTRACTIONS 3, EXCURSION 3, WALK 4**.

Lindos

Lipsi: A small but beautiful island midway between Leros and Patmos. A 30 min walk south of the harbour is Platia Yialo, the island's best beach. Other beaches can be found at Katsadia and Lendori. A drinkable wine is produced on the island, and there are a number of inexpensive tavernas along the harbour waterfront.

Mandraki Harbour: Rhodes Town. Two columns bearing bronze deer, the emblem of Rhodes, stand at the entrance to the harbour which the Colossus of Rhodes (see **A-Z**) is reputed to have straddled. Along the mole protecting the west side of the harbour are three windmills which used to provide flour for the cargo ships. The Fort of St. Nicholas, built in 1446, still guards the end of the pier but the traffic today is mainly pleasure craft. See **WALKS 1 & 3**.

Moni Skiadi: 50 km from Rhodes Town. Near the village of Messanagros above Apolakkia Bay in the southwest of the island, this monastery was founded in the Byzantine era and restored in the 18thC. Although now somewhat delapidated, the church contains several interesting frescoes. See **ATTRACTIONS 2, EXCURSION 4**.

Moni Tsambika: 29 km from Rhodes Town. Close to the summit of Mount Tsambika, this Byzantine cloister dates from the 14thC and consists of five whitewashed cells. From outside there is a wonderful view out to sea. Each year on 7 Sep., childless women make a pilgrimage here. See **ATTRACTIONS 2, EXCURSION 3**.

Monolithos: 80 km from Rhodes Town. A short distance southwest of the village of Monolithos is Monolithos Castle, perched on top of a 260 m-high rock, from where the Knights (see **A-Z**) kept watch over the sea and surrounding countryside. There is a small whitewashed chapel, still used, inside the ruins, and you can see the old walls surrounding the rocky plateau of the summit. Access to the castle is via a flight of stone steps. See **ATTRACTIONS 3, EXCURSION 2**.

Monte Smith: 2 km from Rhodes Town. The ancient Hellenistic town of Rhodes is located on the eastern slopes of Monte Smith. There are some remains of the town, including a reconstructed stadium and the partially restored Temple of Apollo. The hill, originally known as Mount Agios Stephanos, has been known as Monte Smith since the time of the Napoleonic Wars, when the English admiral Sydney Smith, used it as an observation point. See ATTRACTIONS 3.

Mount Ataviros: This is the highest mountain on the island, with a peak of 1215 m. At the summit are the ruins of a sanctuary dedicated to Zeus, and also the small Church of St. John the Evangelist. The views from the summit are superb. Guides for the ascent can be hired in Embonas (see **A-Z**). On the lower eastern slopes towards Agios Isidoros are the remains of a monastery, Agios Iannis Artamitis, which flourished between the 12th and 14thC. See EXCURSION 2.

Museum of Decorative Arts: Rhodes Town. Housed in what used to be the arsenal, there are displays of traditional Dodecanese (see **A-Z**) costumes, furniture, ceramic plates from Lindos (see **A-Z**), and carved sea chests. On the right of the entrance is a pile of cannonballs stacked ready for use during the siege of 1522. See ATTRACTIONS 1, WALK 1.

New Market (Nea Agora): Rhodes Town. Situated in the New Town near Mandraki Harbour (see **A-Z**), this impressive polygonal building encloses a courtyard with food stalls and small shops. On the west side are butchers and vegetable merchants. The main fish market is in the domed building in the centre and is only open in the early morning. There are lots of cafés and bars in the market, with tourists mainly seated on the harbour-side and locals in the market itself. See WALK 3.

Nisyros: Mandraki is both a charming village and the main port of this island. It lies beneath the monastery of Panagia Spiliana, which contains the small 10thC Chapel of Holy Mary. The castle was built by the Knights (see **A-Z**). However, the island's main attraction is the volcanic crater with its hot sulphur vents. Situated close to the crater is the picturesque village of Nikia. In Loutra there is a spa of sulphurous spring water. There is an interesting view of the surrounding area from Agios Theodori. See ISLANDS.

Palace of the Grand Masters: Rhodes Town. This 300-room castle with moats, drawbridges, watch towers and battlements dates from the late 14thC and served as the home of the Grand Master of the Knights of St. John (see **Knights**). It survived the 1522 siege reasonably well, only to be blown up in 1856 by an explosion in an ammunition store. It was rebuilt by the Italians in the early 20thC and used as a seat of Italian government, as well as for entertaining King Victor-Emmanuel II and Mussolini. The palace is worth visiting, if only for one of the finest collections of Hellenistic and early-Byzantine mosaics. See ATTRACTIONS 1, WALK 1.

Patmos: The island is associated closely with St. John, as it was here that the Book of Revelations was written in AD 95. The Monastery of the Apocalypse, 2 km south of Skals, is on the spot where the book is supposed to have been written. The main monastery dedicated to the saint is that of St. John the Divine, and pilgrims come from all over Europe to worship here at Easter. See ISLANDS.

Petaloudes: 20 km from Rhodes Town. From mid June to Sep. the valley at Petaloudes is inundated with thousands of small, brightly-coloured butterflies (*Callimorpha quadrippunctaria*), probably originating in Turkey. One explanation for this concentration is that the butterflies are attracted by the strong scent of benzoin, a resin produced by one of the variety of trees which grow in the valley. The walk is through a scenic valley with well-constructed bridges and paths, and benches at the main viewing points. There is a small shop selling souvenirs and postcards, and a taverna 350 m from the car park. The area is a very popular tourist destination in high season. See ATTRACTIONS 3, EXCURSION 1.

Prophitas Ilias: The third-highest mountain on the island, at 780 m, it is clad in a forest of pine, cypress and old cedar trees. There are some marked walks leading up the mountain which pass two Italian-built, Alpine-style hotels and a monastery. There is a military installation at the summit, to which there is no admission and photography is prohibited. See EXCURSION 2.

Rhodes New Town (Nea Chora): To the northwest of the Old Town (see **A-Z**) in the area around the harbour, the New Town was first developed in the 16thC during the Turkish occupation, when Greeks were forbidden to live in the walled town and built settlements outside its walls. Most of the present-day buildings date from the Italian occupation. The New Town contains few buildings of interest, but is the administrative area, with the post office, Town Hall and the main banks. The most outstanding structure is the Governor's Palace, which resembles the Doge's Palace in Venice and looks strangely out of place here. See WALK 3.

Rhodes Old Town: At the end of the 5thC BC the three ancient cities of the island of Rhodes united to form a fourth, Rhodes, on the northern tip of the island. Rhodes Town flourished as a centre of Hellenistic culture. It has also experienced life under Roman, Byzantine, Italian, Crusader and Ottoman Turk rule. The major architectural influence is from the period of the Knights of St. John (1309-1522). The Knights (see **A-Z**) reconstructed and strengthened the already-existing ramparts to better fortify the town against the Turks. Set in the shape of an irregular square, the walls are up to 12 m thick in places. Each Tongue of the Knights was responsible for the defence of a separate section of the walls. The Turks were later to add thick, round towers called *koule*. Of the gates in the walls, the three that you are most likely to see, and which are also the most impressive, are: Eleftheria (Liberty or Freedom) Gate – The usual entrance to the Old Town and closest gate to Mandraki Harbour (see **A-Z**). It was reconstructed in the 1920s and named in 1947 to commemorate the reunification of Rhodes with Greece. The gate leads into Platia Simi and to the ruined Temple of Aphrodite. On the seaward side is the older (15thC) St. Paul's Gate, a narrow gate leading onto the commercial harbour.

Amboise Gate – The nearest gate to the Palace of the Grand Masters (see **A-Z**). It is the most spectacular of the gates, extending across the inner and outer moats, and was built in 1512 by Grand Master Aimerie d'Amboise, whose coat of arms is carved on the outer part of the gate.
Marine Gate – This links the eastern part of the Old Town to the commercial harbour. It is a grand structure with a high arch, and tall machicolated towers on either side decorated with white marble bas-reliefs of the Virgin Mary, St. Peter and St. Paul. There is also the coat of arms of Pierre d'Aubusson, the 15thC grand master who played a major part in strengthening the town's defences against the Turks. See **ATTRACTIONS 1 & 2, WALKS 1 & 2.**

Rodini Park: 3 km from Rhodes Town. This wooded park is situated on the slopes leading up to a limestone plateau and approached via a tunnel carved through the rock. Within the park is a 3rdC BC necropolis with Doric columns, traditionally known as the Tomb of the Ptolemies. It is also thought to have been the site of the Rhodes School of Rhetoric, where many famous figures in Greek and Roman history (including Julius Caesar) studied. Today it is a pleasant area for a walk, with attractions such as an orchestra playing (in the summer) bouzouki (see **A-Z**) and international music, and an enclosure with Rhodian deer. See **EXCURSION 1**.

Simi: The island used to be prosperous through sponge-fishing and ship-building. It was here that the Allied takeover agreement was signed after World War II. Ghialos, the main port on the northern side of the island, was declared an historical site in 1971. White houses surround the bay and many are designed in a neoclassical style but actually date from the 19thC. Choro is the fortified area on the hill behind Ghialos and its houses were incorporated within its walls to protect them from marauding pirates. There are some 500 steps up from the harbour to Choro. When a boat enters the bay, the bells of the 12thC church are rung. Panorimitis is the site of a magnificent 18thC monastery dedicated to St. Michael and is accessible by boat. See **ISLANDS**.

Suleiman Mosque: Rhodes Town. Erected in honour of Suleiman the Magnificent's conquest of the Knights (see **A-Z**) in 1522 and built on the site of the Church of the Apostles, this is the largest mosque on Rhodes. It has a stone minaret, red plaster walls and a bright airy interior. See **ATTRACTIONS 2, WALK 2**.

Tilos: The main town (which has pleasantly uncrowded beaches) is the port of Livadia. Megalochorio is 8 km north. Its name means 'big town', though it only has around 150 inhabitants. The village is dominated by a Venetian castle. Many tourists come to Tilos for the festival at the monastery of Agios Panteleimonos on 25-27 July. See **ISLANDS**.

Turkish Quarter: This is the area of Rhodes Old Town (see **A-Z**) which the Turks moved into when they invaded Rhodes in 1522. Decorated doorways, arched windows high in the walls, and courtyards are typical of the area. They built the Suleiman Mosque (see **A-Z**) to commemorate the capture of the island, and opposite is the Turkish Library. The Turkish Baths or Hamam on Archelaou/Ippodamou streets is now known unromantically as the Municipal Baths (0500-1900, women to the right, men to the left; 500 Drs). See **WALKS 1 & 2**.

Simi

Marine Gate, Rhodes Old Town

Accidents & Breakdowns: The standard procedure should be employed if you are unfortunate enough to be involved in an accident; you should exchange names, addresses and insurance details. The police (see **A-Z**) are unlikely to intervene unless someone has been injured, in which case it is wise to contact your consulate (see **A-Z**). Car hire companies will supply emergency service details in the event of the breakdown of one of their vehicles. For road assistance, tel: 104. See **Driving**, **Emergency Numbers**.

Accommodation: Rhodes Town and the northeast and northwest coasts are the principal sites of hotel accommodation. A detailed list of hotels is available from the office of the Association of Hotels, Rhodes, located behind the tourist office in Makariou Street. The tourist office can advise on accommodation but cannot make reservations. Hotel categories range from Luxury (Lux) through to family-run accommodation (D or E). Prices range from over 20,000 Drs to 3000 Drs per night. There are no hotels in Lindos but there are plenty of rooms to let, most of good quality. The tourist office in the main square in Lindos will give you details and arrange bookings. *Domatia* (private houses) provide good, and usually cheap, accommodation. Details of these establishments can be obtained from the tourist police. See **Camping**, **Youth Hostels**.

Airport: Rhodes International Airport is located at Paradisi, 12 km along the west coast road from Rhodes Town. The airport has all the usual facilities, including a tourist office. Travel to Rhodes Town is by bus or taxi. Buses can be caught on the main road outside the entrance to the airport (200 Drs to Rhodes Town). Taxis are reasonably priced and plentiful.

Baby-sitters: Some hotels may be able to arrange child-minding services if given sufficient advance notice. Children often stay up late and are accepted in most establishments if they are well behaved. See **Children**.

Banks: See **Currency**, **Money**, **Opening Times**.

Best Buys: There are growing numbers of outlets for ceramics around the island. Plates and wall plaques, for example, are particularly attractive, often incorporating gold leaf and Moorish-inspired designs. Leatherwork is to be found throughout the Greek islands and sandals, handbags, belts and clothing are good value and well made. There are also a surprising number of fur shops in Rhodes Town, which is difficult to contemplate in the heat and at odds with politically correct dressing! There are also a lot of umbrella shops, equally out of place, but worth a look if you are heading back to a north European winter. The Ministry of Culture sells casts and reproductions of Classical works of art from Ippoton Street, Rhodes Old Town, which are beautifully made though expensive. Rugs and carpets made in cotton and wool locally and on the mainland make interesting souvenirs, and arrangements can be made to ship them home for you. Sponges are sold from stalls around the harbour in particular. Embroidered tablecloths, blouses and handkerchiefs, crocheted mats and supposedly hand-knitted sweaters are also widely available. See SHOPPING 1 & 2, **Markets**, **Shopping**.

Bicycle & Motorcycle Hire: Although bicycles can be hired, many of the island's attractions are too far away to reach in a day's cycling. Mopeds for hire on Rhodes usually include only third-party insurance which does not cover damage to either the rider or the bike. Full insurance is therefore advisable as the roads, particularly to the south of the island, can be hazardous. Hire shops, for both bicycles and motorcycles, can be found throughout Rhodes Town, at Faliraki, Trianda, Lindos and several smaller beaches. A bicycle costs around 1400 Drs per day and a moped from 3500 Drs per day. No licence is required for vehicles up to 125cc. Motorcycles are not allowed in towns 1400-1630 or after 2300, and can cost up to 11,000 Drs per day.

Boats: The main passenger ferry port is the commercial harbour located to the east of Rhodes Old Town. There are scheduled stopping services to all the Dodecanese islands (see **ISLANDS**), as well as to Piraeus, Crete and Turkey. The journey time varies depending on the number of ports of call. There is a speedier hydrofoil service, known as the 'Flying Dolphin', with services in high season to Kos, Simi and

Mandraki Harbour

Patmos. At present there is a free service to Kastellorizo (see **A-Z**), as the Greek government is trying to promote tourism there. From Mandraki Harbour there are excursions and day-trip sailings, including services to other parts of the island, such as Lindos. Contact the tourist office for details of where to obtain information about the various ferry operators, their schedules and their prices. There are daily sailings to Halki (see **A-Z**) from Kamiros Skala, which is on the west coast of the island.

Budget: 1993 prices. You will pay more in Rhodes Town at pavement cafés than you will at out-of-town tavernas.

Breakfast	from 800 Drs per person
Lunch (Greek salad and drink)	from 1000 Drs
Fresh orange juice	from 300 Drs
Coffee and bun	from 500 Drs
Beer (large Amstel)	350 Drs
Retsina (0.5 l)	500 Drs

Buses: These are the cheapest method of travelling around the island. There are three main departure points in Rhodes Town: Sound and Light Square, opposite the New Market, for routes around the town; buses do a circuit every 30 min but the town is so small that distances are easily walked, except to Monte Smith (see **A-Z**). Papagou Street (KTEL buses) for the east coast. Averof Street (RODA buses) for the west coast. Within the city limits a ticket costs 250 Drs and a day pass is available for 800 Drs. Rhodes to Lindos costs 750 Drs one way. Tickets are bought on the bus before departure. The usual bus services do not apply on Sun. and holidays, and in high season the buses get very crowded.

Cameras & Photography: Films, batteries and video tapes are available from photographic kiosks, music shops and larger stores, although items tend to be more expensive in the latter. Photography is allowed in most museums. However, because of the proximity to Turkey, there is a large military presence on Rhodes, so be careful to obey the 'No photography' signs.

Camping: Unauthorized camping is forbidden on Rhodes. There is one camp site with amenities including shops, sporting facilities and nightlife. Faliraki Camping is outside Faliraki village. It costs 950 Drs per person per day.

Car Hire: Renting a car is an ideal method of visiting the island's sights at leisure. In summer it is advisable to book at least one day in advance. Most of the major agencies are represented in Rhodes Town. In addition, there are many local agencies which may offer discounts. Local hire details include a minimum age of 23, presentation of a valid international licence and, occasionally, presentation of a passport. It is advisable to ensure that comprehensive insurance is included. Many agencies require an accident damage deposit of up to 20,000 Drs. Major agencies usually waive this deposit if payment is made by credit card. Some agencies also have restrictions concerning driving on mountain roads, so you should check in advance about this. See **Driving**.

Chemists: Known as *pharmakia* and identified by their sign of a red, blue or green cross on a white background. As a rota system is in operation there is always one chemist open day or night. The name and address of the duty chemist can be obtained from the hotel desk or by contacting the tourist police. See **Health**.

Children: Restaurants welcome children and will provide small portions. Bear in mind that by stacking the ubiquitous plastic chairs you can raise your child to table height. There are few attractions specifically aimed at youngsters, though the larger hotels are beginning to provide diversions and facilities such as water slides, for example at Aqua Adventure between the Pegasos and Calypso hotels at Faliraki. Take extra care of fair young skin in the very strong sunlight and give children plenty to drink to counteract dehydration. See **Baby-sitters**.

Cinemas: Several cinemas can be found in Rhodes New Town. General-release films are usually shown with subtitles in Greek. In Faliraki there are several video clubs showing up-to-date films in English.

Climate: Rhodes is the island of Helios, the sun-god. As befits this title, eight months of sunshine are usually recorded between April and Jan. Feb. and Mar. are considered rainy months. In spring and autumn the temperature drops considerably at night but is pleasant during the day. In the summer temperatures can soar on the east coast, while the west coast tends to be cooler due to the prevailing breeze.

Complaints: In the event of a general complaint about a hotel or restaurant, the tourist police can be contacted to arbitrate, tel: 27423.

Consulates:
UK – 23 25 Martiou Street, Rhodes Town, tel: 24963.
Republic of Ireland – 7 Vas. Konstandinou Ave, Athens, tel: 7232771.
Australia – 15 Messogion Ave, Athens, tel: 7757651.
Canada – 4 Ioannis Gennadiou Street, Athens, tel: 7239511.
New Zealand – 15-17 Tsocha Street, Athens, tel: 64103115.
USA – c/o Voice of America Radio, Rhodes, tel: 24731.

Conversion Chart:

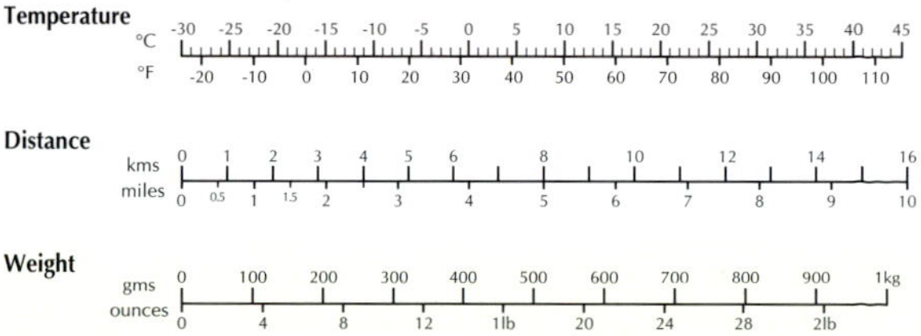

Credit Cards: See **Money**.

Crime & Theft: The general rules of caution apply. Always keep money, traveller's cheques and passports in the hotel safe. In the event of a theft, contact the police (see **A-Z**) at Ethelondon Dodekanissiou, Rhodes New Town, tel: 100. See **Consulates**, **Insurance**.

Culture: Enjoy the colourful costumes of the Folk Dance Theatre group located at Andronikou Street in Rhodes Old Town (season starts 1 May). The authentic atmosphere is further enhanced by the open-air stage designed to reflect the courtyard of a village house. Descriptive texts on the dances can be obtained at the entrance. Although expensive at 1500 Drs, it is an interesting spectacle (2115 Mon.-Fri.; tel: 20157/29085). Ancient Greek and Roman tragedies are enacted by the Dodecanese Theatre Company at the Ancient Theatre on Monte Smith. The season's programme also includes modern plays, as well as Classical, contemporary and folk music recitals. Details can be obtained from the tourist office. The Son et Lumière (Sound and Light) show takes place in a municipal garden below the Palace of the Grand Masters (entrance on Papagou Street, opposite the New Market). The 60 min show gives an account of the Turkish siege of Rhodes in 1522. Performances in English take place Mon.-Fri. Check the notice on the gates for times, which change from day to day in high season. The cost is around 1000 Drs.

Temple of Lindian Athena, Lindos

Currency: The drachma (Drs) is the Greek monetary unit.
Coins – 5, 10, 20, 50 and 100 Drs.
Notes – 50, 100, 500, 1000 and 5000 Drs.
See **Money**.

Customs Allowances:

UK/EC	Cigarettes	Cigarillos	Cigars	Tobacco	Still Table Wine	Spirits/Liqueurs	Fortified Wine	Additional Still Table Wine	Perfume	Toilet Water	Gifts & Souvenirs
Duty Free	200 *or*	100 *or*	50 *or*	250 g	2 *l*	1 *l* *or*	2 *l* *or*	2 *l*	60 cc/ml	250 cc/ml	£32
Duty Paid	800	400	200	1 kg	90 *l*	10 *l*	20 *l*				

With the Single European Market, travellers are subjected only to highly selective spot checks. The red and green channels no longer apply within the EC. There is no restriction, either by quantity or value, on *duty-paid* goods purchased in another country, provided they are for the purchaser's *own personal use* (guidelines have been published). If you are unsure of certain items, check with the customs officials as to whether payment of duty is required.

Disabled People: Very few hotels have lifts so check this carefully before leaving home. Parts of Rhodes Old Town are cobbled and make life extremely uncomfortable for wheelchair-users and impossible for anyone with walking difficulties. Many of the roads and paths are also very rough and kerbs very high. If you come across a ramp, it will be a happy coincidence, not a thoughtful provision. But even though you may find people staring, probably because disablement is rather hidden in Greece, they are very helpful about moving chairs in restaurants and helping with steps. See **Health**.

Drinks: In the past Rhodian wines were famous throughout the Greek world. They are still of good quality, especially the dry white Ilios or the dry red Chevalier de Rhodes (1250 Drs per bottle). Retsina is the wine of Greece itself, a pine resin-flavoured white wine which is best drunk icy cold. Ouzo, an aniseed spirit, is usually drunk with water added. Metaxa and Botrys are Greek brandies which are generally sweeter than the French equivalent. The local eau de vie is called *oumi* and is similar to raki, found in other parts of Greece. Lager-type beers are popular, the Greek brand being Fix, though Amstel, brewed under license, is the most widely available. Tap water is good. A request for coffee will usually result in instant coffee (*nes*), except in country areas where Greek coffee will be served, usually with a glass of water. Greek coffee is strong and served in tiny cups. It can be drunk *gliko* (sweet), *metrio* (medium) or *sketo* (plain). When ordering, specify *nes*, instant coffee; *filtro*, filtered; or *elliniko*, Greek.

Driving: An EC or international driving licence and third-party insurance are obligatory. Green Card insurance is recommended. The use of seat belts is compulsory. There are two main routes on Rhodes. The

east coast road through Lindos and down past Katavia is tarred and in good condition. The west coast road through Ialyssos and Kamiros to Katavia is tarred but there are sharp bends. A network of smaller roads links the two main routes but very few of these are tarred, so low speeds and care are needed. The island is well signposted only on the main east and west coast routes and a road map is essential. See **Accidents & Breakdowns**, **Parking**, **Petrol**.

Drugs: The authorities do not differentiate between hard and soft drugs and are strict on anyone carrying even small amounts of hashish. Drug trafficking can mean life imprisonment.

Eating Out: There is no shortage of eating places in Rhodes and everyone should find something to suit their taste and their pocket. Possibilities range from *haute cuisine* in one of the up-market tourist hotels to souvlakia bought from a stall and eaten on the street. In tavernas (usually family-run, cheaper and more informal than restaurants) you can go into the kitchen and decide what you want. Fish, while abundant, is generally more expensive than meat. The menu shows two prices, with and without service, and you pay the higher one. Desserts are not normally served in restaurants (though many serve them for tourists). You should ideally retire to a coffee house or *zacharoplasteion* for a coffee and something sweet after a meal. Many around Rhodes are open all day and until late at night. See **RESTAURANTS 1-3**, **Food**.

Electricity: 220 V. Two-pin plugs are used; adaptors are available in most electrical retailers.

Emergency Numbers:

Police	100
Fire	199
Ambulance	166
First aid	22222
Hospital emergency	2555
Tourist police	27423

Events:

February: Carnival with floats and fancy dress at Rhodes Town, Archangelos, Apolona and Kamiros Skala.
7 March: Union Day, the celebrations to mark the Dodecanese (see **A-Z**) becoming part of Greece.
1st Mon. of Lent: A fasting day when some eat only potatoes and garlic.
Good Fri.: Silent processions through Rhodes Town.
Easter Sat.: Evening Mass and fireworks, and candles at 2400.
1 May: Doorways decorated with garlands of flowers.
June: The last ten days mark the summer celebrations, with beauty competitions, folk dancing and singing, with the participation of tourists.
July: The first week is Naval Week, with boat races, open-air concerts and fireworks. At the end of the month there is a religious festival with athletics at Agios Soulas near Soroni on the west coast.
August: An exhibition of arts and crafts at Kremasti, with processions and dancing on Assumption Day (15 Aug.). This is the biggest festival in the Dodecanese and lasts for one week.
8 September: Nativity of the Virgin. The day before, childless women make a pilgrimage to Moni Tsambika to pray for fertility.
28 October: National Day.
14 November: Feast of the patron saint of Rhodes, Konstantinos Idertos, when priests from all over the Dodecanese gather at Rhodes.

Food: Popular Greek dishes that are available include: moussaka (minced meat, aubergine, potato and béchamel sauce); pastitsio (minced meat in béchamel sauce); dolmes (stuffed vine leaves); keftedes (spicy meatballs); souvlakia (chunks of meat cooked on a spit, often served in pitta bread with salad); taramasalata (fish roe and cream); tzatziki (cucumber, yoghurt and garlic); mezes (a range of small dishes served to accompany drinks or as a starter). Fish dishes are abundant on Rhodes and are served in a variety of ways. Fish is priced by weight and is more expensive than meat. See **RESTAURANTS 1-3**, **Eating Out**.

Guides & Tours: There are plenty of accompanied tours on offer throughout the island, to Lindos (by land or sea), Rhodes Town or Petaloudes, to a Greek evening with food, wine and entertainment, and to the ancient sites. Package holiday companies will arrange these for you and you will find agents in all the resorts; for example, Ibiscus Tours, 11 Ierou Lochou Street, Rhodes Town. Several of the major sights have regular guided tours in different languages; for example, the Palace of the Grand Masters and the ramparts.

Health: The most common ailments are caused by overindulgence of sun and food. One problem can be the pink and purple jellyfish. If you are stung, rub the wound with ammonia and if problems persist see a doctor. EC members do have reciprocal health coverage but private holiday insurance (see **A-Z**) is a good idea as the Greek service is not as extensive as that in the UK.
Hospital (24 hr outpatient clinic) – Evrou Stavrou, tel: 25555.
English-speaking doctor – Dr Sotiriou, 85 Amerikis Street, Rhodes Town, tel: 29333 (emergency number, tel: 30455).
English-speaking dentist – Dr Papazacharias, 32 Polytechniou Street, Rhodes Town, tel: 24516.
See **Chemists**.

Insurance: Health and personal accident insurance is essential, particularly if you intend to hire a car or motorcycle. Travel insurance against theft and loss of property and money is also advisable. Obtain this sort of insurance before you leave home; your bank or travel agent will give advice. See **Crime & Theft**, **Driving**, **Health**.

Laundries: Hotel staff can usually arrange contact with the numerous dry-cleaners and laundries located in Rhodes New Town. There are Launderettes at all the major resorts.

Lost Property: If you have lost or found any property, tel: 23294.

Markets: There is a large food market on Sat. morning on the way into Rhodes Town by way of the east coast road. Fish is sold direct from the boats below the walls of the Old Town, and there is a daily food market at Palia Agora in the Old Town. Stalls are occasionally set up selling embroidered goods, sponges and other tourist goods near the road to Moni Tsambika, and on fiesta days villagers will move their wares out onto the streets. See **New Market**, **Shopping**.

Money: Well-known credit cards such as American Express, Visa and MasterCard are accepted at the larger shops or car hire agents in Rhodes Town. Small hotels, most petrol stations, average restaurants and small shops usually accept cash only. Cash can be obtained using a credit card at the Commercial Bank of Greece, Sound and Light Square, Rhodes Town. Other banks are the National Bank of Greece and the Credit Bank of Greece, both in Kypros Square. Sterling and dollar traveller's cheques are easily changed at banks and bureaux de change. Banks will not make a charge, but expect to pay at least 2% at *cambios* and at hotel reception desks. Do not expect small retailers to accept traveller's cheques. See **Currency**, **Opening Times**.

Newspapers: Foreign papers and magazines arrive the day after publication and can be found in the bookshops opposite the post office, around the Mandraki area, in larger hotels and at kiosks. See **What's On**.

Nightlife: Most of the discos, bars and nightclubs are to be found in Rhodes New Town in the Academias area. There is a lively nightscene in Ixia, Lindos and Faliraki. See NIGHTLIFE, **Bouzouki**, **Cinemas**.

Opening Times:
Shops – 0800-1430 Mon., Wed. & Sat., 0800-1300 Tue., 1700-2100 Thu. & Fri. Shops remain open all day in the tourist season.
Banks – 0800-1400 Mon.-Fri., winter (some open in the afternoon). 0800-1300, 1700-2100 Mon.-Fri., 0800-1300 Sat., summer.
Nightclubs – Mostly close at 0300.
Restaurants – Many open for breakfast at 0800 and stay open all day in the tourist season. Otherwise, lunchtime 1100-1500, dinner 1800-very late. Serving usually stops at 2400.

Orientation: Rhodes Town is situated on the northern tip of the island. From this point there are two possible routes down the island: the east coast road through the popular resort of Faliraki to Lindos and Katavia in the south; or the west coast route, less busy once past the built-up resort of Trianda Bay, to Apolakkia, three-quarters of the way down the coast. A good tarred road now almost completely encircles the island, with only about 10 km of rough road left to the south of Apolakkia. The interior of the island is mountainous with isolated villages and wooded hills and valleys. The highest mountain is Mount Ataviros (see **A-Z**), which lies half way down the west coast.

Sindrivani Square, Rhodes Old Town

Parking: Parking in Rhodes New Town is difficult and thick yellow lines indicate no-parking areas. If you are driving in from one of the resorts, leave your car below the walls of the Old Town, around the port area where the parking is free, but get there early. Vehicles are not allowed into the Old Town. In other areas of the island parking is not a problem. Do not leave belongings on car seats and make sure your car is locked. See **Driving**.

Passports & Customs: There is no visa requirement for visitors from EC countries and there is no limit on the length of stay. There is also no limit on the amount of money brought into the country in foreign exchange, but if it exceeds $500 it should be declared. It is illegal to export more money than is imported. If money is received from abroad while in Greece, proof of the bank transaction must be produced. See **Customs Allowances**.

Petrol: There are petrol stations in Rhodes Town, along main roads and in the larger villages. They close at 1900 but one always remains open on a rota basis. The address of the open station can be found in newspapers, at taxis ranks or by tel: 27423. Top up before you head off into the mountains or into the less developed south of the island. Super costs 202 Drs per litre, unleaded 190 Drs per litre and diesel 138 Drs per litre (1993 prices). You will be served at most petrol stations and few accept credit cards. See **Driving**.

Police: There are two branches of the police force: the general police and the tourist police. The general police have green uniforms and deal with civilian problems, while the tourist police have blue uniforms and assist with tourist-related problems such as complaints about over-charging. They wear badges indicating which languages they speak. Police headquarters is near the main post office on Platia Eleftherias, and the tourist police are just inside the Old Town at Arsenal Gate. See **Crime & Theft**, **Emergency Numbers**.

Post Offices: The main post office is located on Platia Eleftherias at Mandraki Harbour (0800-2000 summer, until 1900 winter). A letter to an EC destination costs 120 Drs and a postcard 90 Drs (1993 prices). A poste restante service is also available; you should have mail addressed to you at Poste Restante, Rhodes, Greece. There is also a post office in the Old Town on Orfeos Street (0800-2000 Mon.-Fri., 0900-1800 Sat. & Sun.).

Public Holidays: 1 Jan.; 6 Jan.; 7 Mar.; 25 Mar.; 1st day of Lent; Good Fri.; Easter Mon.; 1 May; 15 Aug.; 28 Oct.; 14 Nov.; 25 Dec.; 26 Dec.

Rabies: Rhodes is officially rabies-free. A certificate is required declaring that any animal brought to the island has been disease-free and has had an antirabies vaccination within the last 12 months.

Religious Services:
Santa Maria Church, 45 Kathopouli Street, tel: 22305 and Dragoumi Street, tel: 26688. 1900 daily, 0800 & 1100 Sun. (May-Sep.); 1800 daily, 0800 & 1100 Sun. (Oct.-April).
St. Francisco Church, Dimocratias Street, tel: 23605. 0700 daily, 1100 Sun. (July-Sep.).
St. Anne's Church, 37 Sotiros Street, Ialyssos/Ixia, tel: 92969. 0900 Sun.
Apollo Beach Hotel, Faliraki. 1800 Sat.
Pegasus Hotel, Faliraki. 1800 Sun.
The Jewish synagogue has a service at 1700 Fri.

Shopping: For everyday shopping Rhodes New Town, particularly around 25 Martiou Street, is an up-to-date centre with branches of major chain stores, good shoe shops, designer boutiques, supermarkets, perfumeries and liquor stores. The Old Town, particularly around Socratous, has largely given itself over to the tourist trade and the prices are competitive because there are so many outlets. The resorts have small supermarkets and a few souvenir shops. See SHOPPING 1 & 2, **Best Buys**, **Markets**, **Opening Times**.

Smoking: Smoking is not allowed in public places, on local or excursion buses, or in most taxis.

Simi

Sports:
Golf – There is an 18-hole golf course at Afandou on the east coast, with a clubhouse, bar and a professional coach. Green fees are 4000 Drs per round, a half-set is 1500 Drs and a trolley 500 Drs.
Horse riding – There are stables between Ialyssos and Filerimos, and between Asgourou and Faliraki, offering hourly rides and half-day treks.
Tennis – There are no public tennis courts, but the larger hotels have courts for their guests.
See **Water Sports**.

Taxis: All taxis are privately owned but there is a new office operating radio taxis, tel: 64712/64736. Tips are not obligatory but customary (see **Tipping**). The main taxi rank in Rhodes Town is in Platia

Alexandria at the south end of Mandraki Harbour, adjacent to the New Market. It is perfectly acceptable to flag down a passing taxi, even if someone has already taken it. This can be disconcerting if you have arranged a fare with a driver and he then stops and picks up someone else, but that is how they work. For the Taxi Owners' Association, tel: 34758.

Telephones & Telegrams: This is a separate service from the post office. Called OTE (Greek Telecommunications Organization), there is one situated on Amerikis Street and another one near Platia Argirokastro (0600-2300 April-Oct.). You can make calls from here or from a call box. Call boxes nearly all take phone cards, which you can buy at kiosks or the OTE in denominations of 1000 Drs or 5000 Drs. Telephone rates are cheaper 2100-0900 and at weekends. You can send telegrams or make international calls from OTE offices. International calls are metered and you pay the cashier after the call. See **Emergency Numbers**.

Television & Radio: There are nine TV channels, including two Greek, one Turkish, one German, one French, one English/American and one continuous news. The radio has news in English, French, German and Arabic 0730-0755. Rodos Sky broadcasts Greek and international music on 99FM, in English 1400-1600 daily.

Time Difference: Rhodes is 2 hr ahead of GMT. The clocks go forward 1 hr in summer.

Tipping: Tipping is considered optional in hotels and restaurants as service is usually included in the bill. The expected rate for taxis is 10%. Chambermaids, barbers, tour guides, waiters or *mikro* (the small boy who helps out) should be tipped 300 Drs.

Toilets: Most public conveniences are clean and well-maintained, and can be found in the New Market, on Alexandrou Papagou, close to the bus terminus; on Orfeos Street between the gates of the Palace of the Grand Masters; and at the clock tower.

Tourist Information: The NTOG office (National Tourist Organization of Greece) is in the centre of Rhodes New Town on Makariou Street, tel: 23255/23655. It is open 0800-1400 and the staff are very helpful. Most speak either English, French or German. They offer free leaflets, newspapers, guidance on choice of hotel, information about rentals, and sightseeing information in general. The City of Rhodes Tourist Information Office is in Rimini Square, Mandraki, tel: 35945, and is open 0800-2000 Mon.-Sat., 0900-1200 Sun. See **Events**, **Guides & Tours**, **What's On**.

Mandraki Harbour

Transport: Buses are the cheapest means of transport. A regular service operates to all the principal villages and main beaches on the island. Mopeds and motorcycles are very popular but they can be dangerous, especially if used on the unsurfaced roads. The most comfortable means by which to explore the island is probably by car. See **Airport**, **Boats**, **Buses**, **Taxis**.

Traveller's Cheques: See **Money**.

Walking: Some agencies are beginning to organize walking tours as a means of exploring the more remote parts of Rhodes. There are routes marked through the countryside by spots of paint on rocks and trees but these cannot always be counted on. Generally speaking, you can walk anywhere except military areas, although there are no large-scale maps available locally. The best months for walking are April-June, Sep. and

Oct. Take the usual precautions, wear protection against the sun, carry food and drink, and wear suitable walking shoes or boots.

Water Sports:
Fishing – No licences are required for line fishing or trolling. The best grounds are said to be off Kamiros Skala, Lindos and Genadi, and boats can be hired locally. Spear fishing is allowed but fish must weigh at least 150 g.
Scuba diving – Only permitted with a recognized school, for example Dive Med at Mandraki Harbour, tel: 280401/33654, or Rhodes Sub-Aqua Centre, tel: 33654.
Windsurfing – Instruction and boards are widely available on both coasts at the major resorts.
Pedalos, surf-skis, and ring and sausage rides are all available, plus water-skiing off the resort beaches.
See **Sports**.

What's On: There are two free English-language newspapers distributed by the tourist offices: the *Rhodes Gazette* which appears seasonally, and the *Rodos News*, which is printed monthly. These are both packed with useful information for the visitor. Flyposters advertise visiting bands and singers, and hotel reception areas and agents in the resorts give details of forthcoming events. See **Culture**, **Events**.

Yachting: Bareboat and skippered charter of sailing or power boats is readily available. Yacht Agency Rhodes International at 26 Amerikis Street, Rhodes Town, tel: 22927, is one of the best. Mandraki Yacht Harbour has good facilities, including water, electricity, all repairs, a 40 ton hoist, slipway, diesel and petrol, chandlers and a boatwatch service. For information, tel: 27690. The Nautical Club of Rhodes is at the southern end of Elli Beach and arranges dinghy and rowing races.

Youth Hostels: There is no youth hostel accommodation on Rhodes. Backpackers tend to stay in private 'rooms', which are the cheapest option from around 2000 Drs per night, or *pensions* at around 2500 Drs per night.

10

This book was produced using QuarkXPress™ and Adobe Illustrator 3.2™ on Apple Macintosh™ computers and output to separated film on a Linotronic™ 300 Imagesetter

Text: William McDowall, with additional information by Hilary Hughes
Photography: Michael Siebert
Electronic Cartography: Susan Harvey Design, and Iain Robinson (1, 20, 22, 26, 28)

First published 1990 Second Edition 1994

Published by HarperCollins Publishers
Printed in Italy by Amadeus S.p.A.
ISBN 0 00 470488-6

Guidebook information is subject to being outdated by changes to opening times, prices, and by fluctuating restaurant standards. Every effort has been made to give you an up-to-date text but the publishers cannot accept any liability for errors, omissions or changes in detail or for any consequences arising from the use of information contained herein.
The publishers welcome corrections and suggestions from readers; write to:
The Publishing Manager, Travel Guides, HarperCollins Publishers, PO Box, Glasgow G4 0NB.

Rhodes Old Town